# The Forgiveness Framework™

## A Trauma-Informed Path for Healing, Freedom, and the Legacy You Leave Behind

Dr. Ansonya Burke

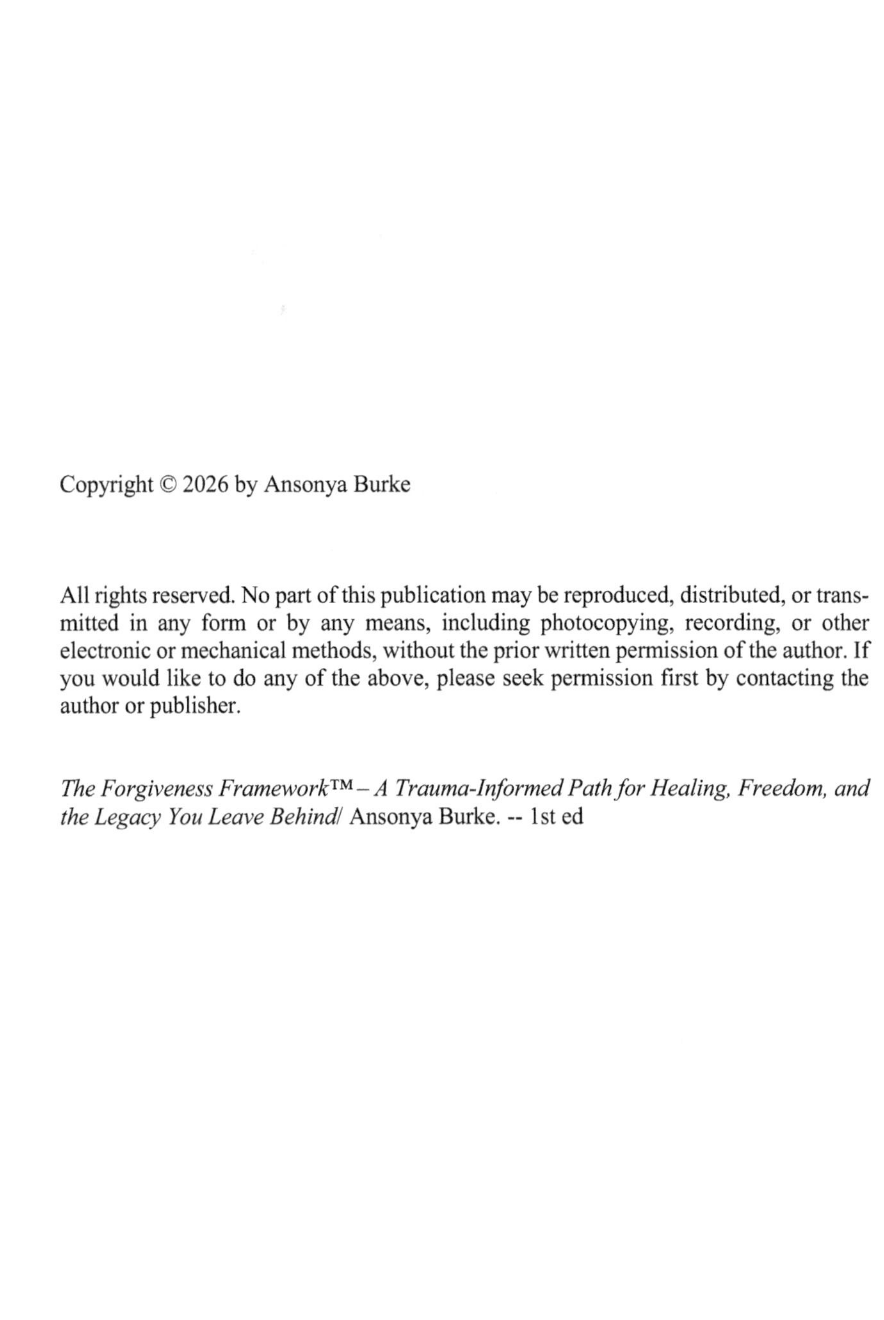



*The Forgiveness Framework™ – A Trauma-Informed Path for Healing, Freedom, and the Legacy You Leave Behind*/ Ansonya Burke. -- 1st ed

# Acknowledgments

To my daughter, Aniyah, and my mother, who stood beside me with gentleness, encouragement, laughter, love, and unwavering faith—you are the tangible proof that generational healing is possible.

To my friends, colleagues, and community of leaders—thank you for walking with me as I learned to balance vulnerability and vision.

To every reader, pastor, professional, and leader who finds themselves here, wondering how to let go with dignity and love—know that you are allowed to honor what was without holding onto what no longer is.

Above all, to God—who patiently taught me that obedience is healing, that boundaries are sacred, and that love without discernment is not loyalty but loss—thank You. You turned my heartbreak into a framework, my pain into purpose, and my story into strength.

Forgiveness changed my story. Resilience sustained my strength. Legacy became my assignment.

With grace, gratitude, and legacy in motion,

– Dr. Ansonya Burke, Founder, The Inner Shift Institute™, Author of *The Forgiveness Framework*™ book series

# Contents

Preface

# The Seeds of Forgiveness

When I began this journey, I thought I was writing about forgiveness. But while going through the process of researching and writing this book, I realized that God was guiding me to write about *legacy*.

To every reader who has walked through pain and hurt, similar to what is described within these pages—thank you for saying "yes" to the work of healing. Forgiveness is sacred labor. It is the rebuilding of trust with yourself, with God, and with those who are ready to see you through a healed lens.

This book was born from my own healing process, when God asked me to return to care for my ex-husband and partner, Red, and I said "yes" through trembling tears. It was a journey that required obedience, courage, and professional partnership. To my therapist, Apostle Shari Eddington, who gently yet truthfully reminded me that "wearing loyalty like a badge of honor is not healing when it's harming you"—thank you. That revelation shifted everything for me.

Through the insight gained from Apostle Eddington, I realized that misplaced loyalty can become emotional bondage disguised as faithfulness. I had to face the truth that loyalty, when given to someone or something that no longer honors your peace, becomes self-betrayal. Healing required me to let go of relationships that could not see me, value me, or honor the woman I was becoming. That was not a rejection of my previous loyalties—it was redirection. It was God whispering, "This season is complete." And though endings are often challenging and can be painful, I learned that release is one of the highest forms of trust.

I have always believed that people come into our lives for reasons, seasons, and lifetimes. Some teach us, some test us, and a few remain as legacy partners in our purpose. But I've also learned that the ones we *choose* are not always the ones God *appoints*. His divine alignments are never accidental; they are assignments wrapped in grace and timing.

Throughout the healing process, the changes within me began to unfold across four dimensions that I now refer to as *The Forgiveness Framework*. First comes *Readiness*, the point at which the heart and nervous system are safe enough to tell the truth about what happened without rushing to resolution. Then comes *Capacity*, the emotional, psychological, and spiritual strength needed to grieve honestly, regulate the body, and hold boundaries without shame. From there, forgiveness moves into *Integration*, where healing is embodied in daily life and no longer performative for the sake of others. And finally, there's *Release*, which is the removal of emotional authority from the wound or the person who caused it. These dimensions shape every stage of this story and every page of this book, which I am honored to share with you.

Foreword

# Pastor Shari Eddington

When I first began working with Dr. Ansonya Burke, it wasn't long before I realized that there was a depth to her story that would one day minister to others. Beneath her poise and professionalism was a woman carrying the burden of pain that had been silenced due to religious expectations forced upon her as a woman of God, but also an unmistakable strength and desire to be all that God has destined for her to become. Over the past three years, I've had the privilege of walking alongside her, as counselor and mentor, watching God methodically transform her from wounded to whole and from survivor to messenger. What unfolds in The Forgiveness Framework is not simply a recounting of events; rather, it is the unveiling of a process. Forgiveness, as Dr. Burke so beautifully demonstrates, is not an act of denial but an act of deliverance. It is the supernatural work of releasing those who hurt you, so that you can reclaim your power from pain, begin to walk in true liberty, and abide in genuine peace. This book chronicles that work in a way that is therapeutic, practical, and relevant, no matter where you are on your forgiveness journey.

In our earliest sessions together, I could sense the tension between the woman she had been and the woman God was calling her to become.

She wanted to be healed, not just for herself, but for the leaders and generations connected to her obedience. That posture of surrender became the soil in which God began to do His greatest work. Over time, I watched her courageously confront memories that had been buried for years. I saw her name the pain that once silenced her, be set free from the rejection that shaped her, and challenge the narratives that once defined her worth. And through every challenge and breakthrough, I witnessed the same miracle I've seen in so many who truly submit to the process of healing: the emergence of wholeness through embracing the love of Christ and their identity in Him.

In this book, Dr. Burke gives you a glimpse into her humanity and gets real about her journey in a way that makes it clear that it was not linear, it was layered, gritty, and even complex at times. If I am transparent, when Ansonya initially spoke with me regarding the possibility of her assisting her ex-husband as his health declined, I was concerned and approached the idea with the utmost caution for my client, as any good therapist would. My initial response was in consideration of the negative toll that the previous visit had on her mentally and emotionally. Therefore, my answer was, "As your therapist, I don't think it will be a good idea". Nonetheless, God began to burden her heart to the degree that she could no longer deny that He was summoning her to serve the very one who deeply hurt her. Not only was God calling her to forgiveness in word, but He was requiring her to forgive in deed. Once, we came to the conclusion that it was indeed divine instruction from the Father for her to go, I told her that I would be here to help her walk through it.

And walk through it we did. There were moments of resistance, questions that had no easy answers, and days when forgiveness felt like an impossible command from God. But I can personally testify that each time, she chose to lean into truth rather than retreat into comfort. She chose not to avoid the challenge, but to go through it by the grace of God. There were indeed times when I had to lead her into some difficult truths, but I watched her pray through the pain, process through the triggers, and pursue peace even when the other party was being unreasonable. That level of obedience is rare. This is the kind of transformation that brings glory to God and highlights the power of divine strength.

I believe that her story will challenge you to see forgiveness in a new light. This book dismantles the myth that forgiveness means forgetting or excusing, but it's the decision to free yourself from the emotional bondage of another person's choices. It is the spiritual act of declaring, "You no longer have authority over my joy, my future, or my faith!" Forgiveness, in its truest form, is a divine exchange. You release others, and in return, God releases you. You relinquish control, and He restores your peace. You stop rehearsing the pain, and He rewrites your story just as God is doing for Dr. Burke. Through these pages, you will not only witness that exchange in Dr. Burke's life, but you will be invited to experience it in your own.

Within *The Forgiveness Framework*, you will encounter practical wisdom rooted in psychological insight, spiritual revelation, and lived experience. You will see how therapy and faith can coexist beautifully, how the principles of emotional health and the truths of Scripture can walk hand-in-hand to produce lasting freedom. This is where my own joy as her therapist collides with my foundation as a Believer: to watch God heal through the tools of the mind, Spirit, and scriptures. If you have ever wondered whether healing is truly possible after betrayal, abuse, or deep disappointment, let this book serve as your answer. Yes, it is possible. Yes, it takes time. Yes, it requires courage, boundaries, and often professional support, but it is also beautifully redemptive.

Dr. Ansonya Burke's journey is proof that God specializes in taking the fragments of our past and forming them into testimonies that set others free. As you read, allow the Holy Spirit to do for you what He has done for her, shine light on the dark places, reveal what still needs to be released, and usher you into the kind of peace that surpasses understanding. May this book meet you where you are, minister to the hidden parts of your soul, and remind you that your story, too, can be redeemed.

– Shari Eddington, MA

Sr. Pastor, Liberate Church Dallas | Therapist & Founder of Real Wholeness Christian Counseling & Coaching | Author *Positioned to Prosper: The Joseph Blueprint for Promotion*

Framework 0

# Why Forgiveness Can Feel Impossible

—✦—

***Before forgiveness can occur, the brain must understand that the threat has passed.***

She was 43 years old the first time she heard someone tell her that her brain had been trying to protect her. She had come to a conference, reluctantly, to hear about forgiveness, not a defense of her life experience. She had spent years hearing *that* word, forgiveness, forced on her like a bill she owed on a debt that she never chose in the first place. "You just have to forgive. Let it go. Move on." Every time she heard those words, something deep inside her tightened, coming from a place she could not fully name, saying, "Not yet."

She did not know it then, but that voice has a name. It lives in a small, almond-shaped region at the center of her brain, nestled deep within the temporal lobe. Neuroscientists call it the amygdala. I call it the sentinel because that is exactly what it is. It is the part of you that never sleeps.

Before we can walk through the 9 Frameworks of Forgiveness, before we can talk about healing, before we can even imagine what freedom might feel like, we must first understand why forgiveness can feel so impossible. Despite what you may have heard, it's not because you are weak, bitter, or lack faith. Forgiveness can be so challenging because your brain is doing exactly what it was designed to do.

So, we start with Framework 0, the foundation beneath every other framework in this book. It is the explanation that finally makes sense of why, even when you wanted to forgive, some part of you could not seem to let go.

What you are about to read is not an excuse but an explanation. And sometimes, that explanation is the first act of compassion we can offer ourselves.

## The Amygdala: Your Brain's Sentinel

Deep inside the human brain is a region that has been present since our earliest ancestors walked the Earth. Long before the development of complex language, philosophy, or moral reasoning, this structure was already doing its job, scanning the environment, detecting threats, and preparing the body to respond.

The amygdala (two small structures, one on each side of the brain) is part of what neuroscientists call the limbic system, the emotional brain. It functions as the brain's alarm system. It processes incoming information at breathtaking speed, faster than conscious thought, faster than words can form, and it makes a single, powerful determination: Is this safe, or is this a threat?

When it identifies a threat of any kind—real or perceived, present or remembered—it activates without your permission. It sends signals throughout the body: cortisol floods the bloodstream, adrenaline surges, the heart rate climbs, and the muscles prepare for fight, flight, or freeze. All of this happens in a fraction of a second before your prefrontal cortex (the thinking, reasoning part of your brain) has even had time to ask, "What is actually going on here?"

***The amygdala does not distinguish between a memory and the present moment. Pain remembered feels like pain happening now.***

Here is what this means for forgiveness. When you have been hurt in ways that shook your sense of safety, your sense of self, or your sense of what is true in this world, that pain does not merely exist as a thought or a memory you can consciously access and then put away. It is encoded in the body, woven into the neural architecture of the brain. The amygdala catalogs it, stores the emotional signature of that experience, and remains on alert for anything that resembles it.

This is why a certain tone of voice can make your chest tighten. This is why a particular phrase, a familiar dynamic, or even a specific smell can pull you back into an experience you thought you had left behind. The amygdala is simply being faithful to its purpose: to keep you alive. This part of the brain was never designed to facilitate forgiveness. And until your nervous system receives a clear enough signal that the danger has passed or the threat is no longer active, your brain will continue to hold that wound as unresolved and still relevant to your survival.

Forgiveness, then, is not simply a moral or spiritual decision. It is also a neurological event. It requires the nervous system to be brought out of survival mode and into a state of safety before the deeper work of healing can take root.

## The Frontal Lobe: The Voice That Reasons

If the amygdala is the sentinel, then the prefrontal cortex, which is housed in the frontal lobe, just behind your forehead, is the counselor.

The prefrontal cortex is the most evolutionarily advanced region of the human brain. It is the seat of executive function: the part of you that can plan ahead, regulate emotion, make complex decisions, and hold two competing realities at once. It is where empathy lives. It is where perspective-taking happens. It is where the capacity for forgiveness itself is rooted.

The prefrontal cortex is capable of remarkable things. It can say, "That person hurt me, and I also understand that they were acting from their own unresolved pain." It can hold the tension between justice and compassion. It can choose with intention to release resentment because freedom matters more than the offense.

However, the prefrontal cortex cannot function at its highest capacity when the amygdala is in control.

***When the alarm is sounding, the counselor cannot be heard. The sentinel will always overrule the counselor until the alarm is turned off.***

Neuroscientists and therapists refer to this phenomenon as emotional hijacking, a term popularized by psychologist Daniel Goleman in his landmark work on emotional intelligence. An emotional hijack occurs when the amygdala's threat response overrides the regulatory, rational function of the prefrontal cortex. In those moments, your capacity for nuanced reasoning, compassionate perspective, and deliberate choice is significantly diminished. You are not broken. You are hijacked.

Think about the moments when someone has told you to "just forgive." Perhaps it was in the immediate aftermath of a wound, when the emotional pain was still fresh and raw. Maybe it was during a conversation that triggered the memory of the hurt all over again. It could have been in a context where you felt pressured, unseen, or spiritually obligated to perform a healing you had not yet experienced. In those moments, your prefrontal cortex was likely not fully online. The amygdala had sounded its alarm. And no amount of willpower or spiritual instruction can override neurological reality.

This is not an excuse to remain in unforgiveness permanently. But it is a profound explanation for why the command to "just forgive" so often fails—because the nervous system has not yet been given the conditions it needs to make forgiveness feel possible.

## The Hijack: When the Body Takes Over

Let me make this personal, because this is not merely academic knowledge. This is the lived experience of every person who has ever tried to forgive and found that their body would not cooperate.

You decide, consciously and sincerely, that you are ready to forgive. You pray. You journal. You tell yourself the story differently. You extend grace in your mind. And then, perhaps in a conversation, a dream, or a quiet moment when a memory surfaces without warning, the wound opens again. The heat rises in your chest. The thoughts you believed you had released come flooding back with a force that surprises even you. You wonder if you were only pretending, if the forgiveness was ever real. You might even start listing all the things you think are wrong with you.

But nothing is wrong with you. You experienced a hijack. The amygdala operates through association. It does not require the original threat to be present in order to activate, only something that resembles the original threat. A tone, a pattern of behavior, a dynamic, an environment, a particular way of being treated that echoes what once harmed you. When those signals appear, the amygdala fires, the stress hormones surge, and the body responds as if the original wound is happening again.

This is the neurological basis of what trauma researchers call a "trigger." And it is one of the primary reasons why unhealed wounds do not simply fade with time. Time does not heal all wounds. What *does* heal wounds is the intentional work of helping the nervous system understand experientially that the threat has passed.

Until that signal reaches the amygdala, it will continue to do its job. It will hold the wound open and keep the body on alert. And it will make the very idea of forgiveness feel not just difficult, but dangerous.

***Your body is not being stubborn. It is being loyal to the version of you that needed protecting.***

## What the Research Confirms

The intersection of neuroscience and trauma is one of the most illuminating fields of study of the past three decades. Researchers have consistently found that traumatic and deeply painful experiences are not stored in the brain the way ordinary memories are stored.

Ordinary memories are processed through a region called the hippocampus, which helps encode experience into a narrative with a beginning, a middle, and an end. This narrative function is precisely what allows us to understand that something happened in the past. It gives the memory a temporal context: that was then, and this is now.

But when an experience is sufficiently overwhelming, the hippocampus can be disrupted. The memory does not get fully processed into a coherent narrative. Instead, emotional, sensory, and physical fragments remain unintegrated, stored in a raw and reactive form. These fragments are retrieved not as clear recollections with defined timestamps, but as feelings, physical sensations, and emotional states that arrive without context, without the reassuring signal that this belongs to the past.

This is why trauma can feel so present. It is not that the survivor is dwelling on the past or refusing to move forward. It is that the brain has not yet been given the experience of safety it needs to complete the processing of that wound. The narrative remains unfinished. The chapter has not been written to its close.

Researcher and author Dr. Bessel van der Kolk has described this reality with one of the most clarifying phrases in modern trauma literature: "the body keeps the score." The body carries what the mind cannot yet hold. The nervous system bears the record of what happened, even when the conscious mind is working hard to let it go. For anyone who has walked through betrayal, abandonment, abuse, profound loss, or relational devastation—this is testimony.

Forgiveness, understood through this lens, is not a single moment of decision. It is the process of a gradual, tended journey back to the self, back to safety, and back to freedom. It requires that the nervous system be honored as a participant in healing, not overridden as an inconvenient obstacle.

## Reframing What Forgiveness Is

Before we move any further together, I need to offer you a reframe because the way forgiveness has often been taught in many contexts has caused tremendous harm to people who were already wounded.

Forgiveness has been presented as instant and obligatory. As the moral and spiritual minimum required of anyone who calls themselves a person of faith, a person of integrity, or a person who "truly" loves. It has been weaponized against survivors who were still in danger. It has been invoked to silence grief, rush healing, and pressure people back into relationships that were still actively harmful.

I want to say clearly, and with conviction: that is not forgiveness but compliance dressed in spiritual language.

True forgiveness, as I understand it (and as the neuroscience confirms), is a process. It is not the denial of pain. It is the dignifying of pain as real, as significant, and as worthy of being fully felt before it is released. It is not the excusing of harm. It is the releasing of the emotional debt that the harm created, not because the offender deserves to be free of consequence, but because you deserve to be free of the weight.

Forgiveness is not reconciliation. You can forgive someone and maintain every boundary that your safety requires. You can forgive someone and never speak to them again. Forgiveness is an internal act of liberation. It does not require the presence, the acknowledgment, or even the awareness of the person who caused the harm.

And crucially, forgiveness cannot be rushed. It cannot be demanded or performed by will alone when the nervous system is still sounding its alarm.

***You cannot think your way to forgiveness. You must be led there through safety, awareness, and the patient tending of the wounded places within you.***

## The Gift of Understanding

I want to return to the woman at the beginning of this chapter who sat in a room, reluctant and wary, hearing for the first time that her brain had been protecting her. That woman is me. And she is you. She is every *person* who has ever sat in the impossible tension between the desire to be free and the inability to force freedom's arrival.

When I first encountered the research on the amygdala, on emotional hijacking, on the neuroscience of trauma, something shifted in me that I can only describe as relief. It gave me permission to be human. It reframed my struggle not as a character flaw or a spiritual failure, but as a biological reality that deserved compassion, not condemnation.

I stopped asking, "Why can't I just forgive?" and began asking, "What does my nervous system need in order to feel safe enough to heal?" That question changed everything, and it will guide us through every framework that follows. Healing can only begin with understanding, self-compassion, and the radical act of treating your own pain as worthy of being known before it is released.

Your brain has been keeping score. Your body has been keeping the record. And now, together, we are going to learn what it means to lay that record down in a process of genuine, tended, hard-won freedom.

## Spiritual Reflection

Take a few moments before moving on. Ask yourself:

- Where in my body do I feel the weight of a wound I have not yet been able to release?
- Has anyone ever demanded that I forgive before I was ready? What did that feel like in my body?

- What would it mean for me to extend compassion to the part of me that has been trying to stay safe?
- What is one thing I now understand about my own healing journey that I did not understand before?

***There is no shame in where you are.***
***There is only the next step, taken when you are ready.***

Framework 1

# When Legacy Meets Pain

— ✦ —

***What you refuse to name will continue to shape you; healing begins the moment truth is spoken.***

There is no healing without honesty. What we refuse to name will continue to occupy sacred space in the heart. Believers will sometimes pray for deliverance from pain while guarding the very thing God is trying to touch. Naming it is not complaining; it is cooperating with your healing. Before restoration comes revelation. We cannot conquer what we will not confront, and we cannot confront what we refuse to acknowledge.

## Wrestling with Destiny

Long before that fateful phone call disrupted my routine, I believed I had finally found stability in my life. My modest home, with its soft, comforting hues, felt like a sanctuary from the chaos that had once defined my marriage. My prayer life had matured, but deep within, I was still haunted by unanswered questions: *Why had I suffered so deeply during my former marriage? Why had God allowed such pain during that time?*

I prayed often, but sometimes my prayers were more about filling the silence than expecting transformation. Yet, God often chooses the quietest moments to stir the waters of our complacency. We may believe our greatest trials are behind us, but He sometimes calls us to face them again for redemption.

That was my reality the evening the phone rang. In one instant, every emotional barrier I had built to protect my peace came crashing down.

## The Haunting Echo of the Past

As I hung up the phone, memories flooded my mind of bitter arguments, broken promises, and loneliness that had nearly undone me. Still, I couldn't ignore the humility and desperation in Red's voice. His plea wasn't just physical; it was spiritual.

I sat with my Bible and opened to the Psalms that night, identifying with David's vacillation between praise and lament. Like David, I was torn, wrestling between empathy and self-preservation. Could God truly be asking me to revisit this pain, not to reopen wounds, but to name and heal them? It was then I realized that God will sometimes lead us back to what hurt us, not to relive it, but to redeem it.

## The Complex Nature of Obedience

Obedience is a dance between divine prompting and human hesitation. There are many who assume that once we've escaped a painful chapter, we will never revisit it. Yet Scripture shows otherwise. Joseph faced his brothers again after they betrayed him. Moses returned to Egypt. Jonah went back to Nineveh. Each faced what once broke them, this time empowered by divine assignment.

So, when God began whispering for me to return to what threatened to break me, I wanted to say, "Why me, Lord? Why can't someone else do it?" But obedience is not a matter of fairness; it's about purpose. Perhaps my history with Red uniquely equipped me to offer a grace no one else could. The thought terrified me, yet peace began to speak: "Name your fear and let faith lead."

The morning I left for the hospital, my hands trembled as I packed. My mother embraced me and offered me a few wise words. "God doesn't waste our pain—remember that." She reminded me that healing often requires revisiting the ground that wounded us with holy courage.

The drive was filled with worship songs that pierced me deeper than before. The lyrics, "Trust and obey," became both my challenge and my confession. Every mile forward was a step deeper into surrender.

When I walked into Red's hospital room, I was unprepared for the flood of emotion. Seeing him frail and broken stripped away the walls of resentment I had built. His eyes spoke more than his words, and were colored with repentance, fear, and a longing for absolution. We sat in silence for a long while, the hum of medical machines filling the space. "Thank you for coming," he finally said softly. That simple sentence carried the heavy load of years of spoken and unspoken pain. In that moment, I understood that healing begins when we name the truth before God. Just as Psalm 51 declares, "You desire truth in the inward parts." Truth begins where denial ends.

## Threading Grace Through Old Wounds

Those early days tested my ability to extend grace without reopening old scars. I had learned through counseling therapy that forgiveness doesn't excuse wrongdoing, but it releases its grip on your soul. Naming my anger, fear, and disappointment aloud was liberating.

Naming is a divine act. In Genesis, God named light, land, and life before their fullness appeared. Naming gives form to what is formless. When I said, "I am angry," peace knew where to go. When I admitted, "I am afraid," faith found its footing. Grace required honesty; wisdom required boundaries. I helped Red when compassion led me, but I stepped away when his words turned harmful. This balance became proof that love and self-protection can coexist.

In the hospital chapel, beneath the glow of a single lamp, I poured out my doubts to the Most High. "Am I walking back into captivity, Lord?" Fear taunted me, but peace replied softly, "You are walking into healing."

Jonah fled from Nineveh because he didn't think they deserved mercy. I realized I, too, resisted extending grace because I didn't believe Red deserved it. But God reminded me that healing is not about who deserves it; it's about who needs it. Naming my resistance—"Lord, I don't want to go"—became my first step toward surrender.

## Baby Steps Toward Reconciliation

Healing was not instant. Some days Red was kind; other days, familiar patterns resurfaced. But each time I named my emotion instead of suppressing it, I regained a sense of peace.

A nurse once said, "He seems calmer when you're here." That statement confirmed what the Spirit was already showing me: that even imperfect obedience becomes a vessel of peace.

When news spread that I had returned to Red's side, reactions varied. Some applauded my strength; others questioned my sanity. One friend asked tearfully, "Do you think you're strong enough to face him again?"

I answered honestly, "Maybe not, but I know God is."

Their questions taught me the importance of safe confession; speaking truth to trusted voices who hold space without judgment. Healing accelerates in environments of honesty, not isolation.

## The Role of Surrender in Obedience

Surrender is active trust. It means naming our fears before God and yielding control of the outcome. Each day, I prayed, "Lord, be my strength." Some days that request steadied me; other days, it was all I could manage.

Through surrender, I discovered a new dimension of obedience: that true healing doesn't always feel like deliverance. It often feels like death to self. Yet resurrection always follows.

Obedience didn't erase hardship. Red's health declined and, for me, exhaustion pressed in. Yet amid the strain, I saw glimpses of grace: Red's first genuine apology, nurses sensing peace in his room, and my own ability to love without losing myself.

God's "yes" rarely guarantees comfort; it guarantees transformation. Each moment of obedience became a seed of healing, not only for Red, but for me.

Returning to Red's side taught me that freedom from past challenges and obstacles isn't just about escaping from pain; it's also the courage to face it with new strength. What I once called closure was really avoidance. What I now call healing began the day I named my truth before God. Healing cannot visit what we hide. When we name our wounds, we reclaim dominion over them. This first act of naming my pain turned my "no" into God's "yes," birthing a new kind of freedom: one rooted not in denial, but in divine honesty.

## Spiritual Reflection

### *Statement of Truth*

What I name, God can heal. What I hide, I continue to hold onto. Naming my pain is not a sign of weakness; it is rooted in strength. When I bring my fear into the light, grace knows where to meet me. Silence once felt like safety, but truth became my freedom. Here is the holy discipline of "naming" that I am learning to practice:

- To name what hurts.
- To name what I fear.
- To name what I long to avoid.

Honesty does not destroy faith; it deepens it. God does not require me to be fearless. He only invites me to be truthful.

*Principle*

Healing begins with revelation, and revelation starts with naming. Before God restores what is broken, He exposes what is hidden. Naming is the first act of obedience because it breaks agreement with denial and restores alignment with truth.

Throughout Scripture, God names before He forms. Light before land. Identity before destiny. When I name my wound, I reclaim authority over it. When I name my fear, faith finds its footing.

Obedience is not always about movement; sometimes it is about confession. Sometimes the bravest thing I can do is say, "Lord, this still hurts."

*Naming Fear as an Act of Faith*

When God invited me to revisit what once wounded me, my first act of obedience was naming my past wounds. Naming fear did not make it disappear. It made it visible. And what becomes visible no longer rules from the shadows.

Like Jonah, I wanted to flee from the place of assignment because it touched old pain. Like Moses, I questioned my adequacy. Like Joseph, I trembled at the thought of facing what once betrayed me. Yet God did not rebuke their fear nor mine; He met it with purpose.

*Therapeutic Lens*

From a clinical standpoint, naming emotions also activates the brain's regulatory systems. When feelings remain unnamed, the nervous system stays locked in survival mode (fight, flight, or freeze), keeping the body braced for danger even when the threat has passed. But when you say, "I am afraid," or "I am grieving," the brain shifts out of alarm and into integration. In simple terms, your body finally gets the message that it is safe enough to process whatever is happening instead of simply enduring it. This is why many people feel both emotional and physical relief after honest conversation or prayer. The weight in the chest softens. The breath deepens. The tension releases. Naming doesn't just clarify the story you've been holding onto; it recalibrates the nervous system as well. In this way, emotional honesty becomes both a spiritual act and a biological invitation to rest.

Spiritually, this aligns with Psalm 32:3-5: "When I kept silent, my bones wasted away... then I acknowledged my sin to You... and You forgave."

In therapy, I learned that naming emotions reclaims control. Spiritually, I learned that naming before God restores the ability for intimacy. I no longer confuse emotional suppression with spiritual maturity. God does not heal what I will not reveal.

## *Case Study*

A woman once brought childhood abandonment into every adult relationship, calling it "wisdom" when it was really unhealed fear. In counseling, she finally said aloud, "I am afraid of being left out or left behind." That confession became the doorway to healing. What she named no longer dominated her choices.

Like her, I discovered that many of my decisions were shaped by wounds I had never named. Once I spoke them aloud before God, they lost their power to rule over me.

## *Tools and Practices*

### Spiritual Tools

- From Scripture, passages like Psalm 51:6, Psalm 32:3–5, and John 8:32 invite you to meditate on truth-telling as an act of spiritual alignment. Psalm 51:6 reminds you that God desires honesty at the deepest level. Psalm 32:3-5 shows the emotional and even physical toll of silence—and the relief that confession brings. John 8:32 reinforces that truth is not just informational; it is liberating.

- Naming Prayer Exercise: Each day, complete the sentence: "Lord, today I feel _____." Allow the emotion to surface without judgment. This signals to both your nervous system and your spirit that it is safe to be honest.
- Emotion Inventory: Write down the situations or memories you avoid. Ask, "What might God want to heal that I have refused to name?"

Therapeutic Practices

- Slow, intentional breathing helps shift the brain out of fight-or-flight, creating space for spiritual reflection.
- Gently challenge thoughts like "I should be over this" with truth: "Healing takes time, and God meets me in my honesty."
- Safe Confession: Share your named emotion with one trusted person. Healing accelerates in supported spaces, not isolation.

### *Reflection and Action*

- What fear have I mistaken for wisdom?
- What pain have I normalized instead of naming?
- Where is God inviting me to speak instead of staying silent?

Write down one truth you have been avoiding. Say it aloud before God. Healing often begins with a sentence.

### *Faith Declaration*

"I declare that truth is my ally and healing is my inheritance. I will no longer hide what God longs to heal. I choose honesty over fear, surrender over silence, and obedience over avoidance. What I name, God redeems."

### *Faith Prayer*

"Lord, teach me the courage of confession and the safety of Your presence. I bring You the truths I once hid and the fears I once buried. Heal what I have avoided, restore what I have misplaced, and redeem what I have named today. I trust You with my truth. Amen."

### *Framework Truth*

Sacred naming is the courage to carry your pain into God's presence and say, "This is where it hurts, and this is where I need You." It is trading silence for surrender and secrecy for trust. What you dare to name no longer rules you from the shadows; it becomes ground where God plants healing. The fear you confess becomes the doorway where faith walks in, and every truth you speak before Him becomes a seed of restoration that reaches beyond this moment and into your legacy.

### *The Forgiveness Framework™ – Readiness*

In this early stage of the journey, The Forgiveness Framework begins with Readiness. This is not about pressure, obligation, or trying to appear "spiritually strong." It is the point when the heart is finally willing to name pain instead of minimizing it. Readiness honors the nervous system, the emotions, and the truth before God. It does not demand forgiveness before the soul has been able to process grief, anger, confusion, or shock. When forgiveness is attempted too early, it becomes performance instead of healing. Readiness allows space to say, "This hurt me. I am not okay yet." In that honesty, forgiveness is prepared for. Readiness becomes the doorway through which authentic healing begins.

Framework 2

# The Weight You Were Never Meant to Bear

—✦—

***You can be compassionate without carrying what was never assigned to you.***

Forgiveness rarely unfolds in a straight line. It's a layered process, a sacred wrestling match between obedience and emotion and between what we know is right and what still feels raw. For me, this wrestling came in the form of an unexpected call that would reopen wounds I thought had long healed.

On this particular day, the phone rang, and for a long moment, I just stared at it. I had already been getting updates from doctors about Red's condition. His disease, polyarteritis nodosa, was back, and this time, it was aggressive. I told myself it was his life, not mine. I had done the hard work of forgiveness. I had found peace.

But on the other end of the line wasn't a doctor's voice; it was Red himself. His tone, once commanding and confident, trembled. "Ansonya… can you come take care of me?"

My chest tightened. My throat closed. My hands began to shake. Decades of betrayal, disappointment, and sleepless nights crashed over me in an instant. *Not again, Lord. Not again.*

That night, I tossed and turned, praying through tears. "Why would You send me back into the place You delivered me from? Haven't I obeyed enough? Haven't I suffered enough?" It felt like I was met with extended silence, followed by a soft voice saying, "You have to go." The second night was much like the first, followed by the same response: "You have to go." By the third night, I felt like Jacob wrestling with the angel—bruised, exhausted, and desperate for another way.

Finally, I did what I always did when life cornered me; I went to therapy. Sitting on the beige couch that had soaked up my tears many times before, I poured it all out: the phone call, the sleepless nights, the divine insistence I couldn't ignore. I waited for my therapist to rescue me, to tell me not to go.

Instead, she said gently, "If God is saying you have to go, then I have to step away. You have to obey if that's what He's speaking. But I will walk this journey with you."

I broke down, sobbing. When the tears finally slowed, she reminded me of something she had told me months before: "Ansonya, you wear resilience like a badge of loyalty. You think staying in hard places proves you're strong. But sometimes, armor becomes your prison."

Her words pierced through every wall I had built. This wasn't just about Red. It was about me and completing a healing that therapy alone couldn't finish. True healing would now require obedience.

## Revisiting Old Territory

Returning to San Antonio to see Red was like a pilgrimage into old pain. It felt like every corner of the city held memories of what once was. The two that stuck out the most were the church where Red and I worshiped and the restaurant where we celebrated anniversaries. The hospital, though, sterile and humming with life and death, was its own spiritual crucible. There, between beeping monitors and cold floors, I realized God was doing something far deeper than mending Red's body. He was refining my soul.

Hospital life taught me about surrender. Nurses rushed in, machines beeped, and doctors updated charts while privacy vanished. It was in those interruptions that grace appeared. I learned to pray between breaths. "Lord, help me." "Thank You, Jesus." "Keep me steady." Prayer became my lifeline, and my faith became mobile, resilient, and adaptive.

Caring for an ex-spouse is a strange paradox. It dredges up memories, challenges identity, and tests boundaries. Years earlier, caregiving had felt like bondage—a tool Red used to control me. But this time, I chose it of my own free will. I could walk away anytime. Still, it was emotionally exhausting. Red's frustrations often became verbal daggers. But rather than absorb his pain, I practiced empathic detachment: acknowledging his suffering without letting it define me. "I understand you're upset, Red, but I'm doing my best to help you," became my steady refrain. His moods often swung like a pendulum. Some days, humor flickered; on others, anger consumed him. I often found refuge in hospital hallways, weeping quietly. "You don't have to do this," a nurse once told me. "You can step away." I could have. But I knew God wasn't calling me to endure abuse; He was teaching me boundaries with compassion. "If you continue to speak to me that way, I will have to step out," I would say calmly. Surprisingly, these boundaries brought him peace—a structure in his unraveling world.

## Forming an Unlikely Community

In waiting rooms, I found unexpected kinship. Strangers became my new companions. These were spouses, parents, and children carrying their own burden of caring for a loved one.

One night, I met Maria, whose husband battled cancer. "He wasn't perfect," she admitted through tears, "but I can't leave him now."

We cried together, prayed together, and parted with renewed strength. Our stories mirrored one another; two women holding grace for men who had once broken our hearts.

Re-entering the city also meant re-joining its faith circles. Churches that once felt judgmental now opened their doors with warmth. Perhaps they hadn't changed; perhaps I had. One midweek service, the pastor preached on Paul's shipwrecks and how sometimes God leads us into storms to refine us and not destroy us. I felt that message touch deep within my soul. Afterward, an elderly woman prayed silently over me. That simple touch reminded me that God was weaving community around my obedience.

Gone were my safe, tidy prayers. Now, I prayed through warfare for healing, salvation, and deliverance. I would also ask God to give the hospital staff wisdom and rest. I even prayed for myself to stay tender and not bitter. Some nights, I read the Book of Job in the chapel, crying until the words blurred together. Like Job, I learned that suffering sometimes carries an unseen invitation to a greater intimacy with God.

## Witnessing Subtle Changes

One evening, something miraculous happened. Red reached for my hand with tears glistening in his eyes. "I'm sorry," he said softly, barely able to get the words out. He then puckered his lips, waiting for me to kiss him. My daughter Aniyah witnessed the moment. His apology was a small gesture, but it was sacred. It was proof that grace had cracked something open in him and me. God was rewriting the ending to a story I thought was already closed.

While caring for Red, friends back home questioned my choices. "How long will you live like this?" they asked. But peace, the same peace that led me here, kept me steady. My actions were purposeful, and I had a mission and perhaps even a ministry. Not to mention, God was healing Red's heart and my own.

What I experienced at Red's bedside was holy endurance. It was agape love in action: patient, kind, but not self-erasing. Like the prodigal story reversed, Red was the one returning, fragile and humbled, and I, the reluctant caregiver, was learning how to love without losing myself. Forgiveness, I discovered, was not reconciliation but revelation.

## Embracing the Mystery

Wrestling is not rebellion; it's an opportunity for revelation. The struggle itself is holy because it births transformation. Stepping back into the fire revealed that God doesn't always lead us away from pain; sometimes, He leads us through it to prove that healing is possible on the other side of obedience. The hospital, though filled with present challenges and past grief, became sacred ground and proof that God redeems even what once burned us.

## Spiritual Reflection

*Statement of Truth*

Some assignments from God do not feel merciful at first; they can sometimes feel too heavy to bear. Obedience is not always gentle; at times, it asks us to return to places we barely survived. But when God calls me back into the fire, He does not send me in alone. He sends me covered in wisdom and anchored in grace.

This is the holy tension I now live in:

- Yes to compassion.
- Yes to obedience.
- No to self-erasure.
- No to absorbing what is not mine to carry.

I am learning that I can show up with love without sacrificing myself or my inner peace again.

### *Principle*

Obedience is faith in motion, but discernment keeps it from becoming destruction. God does not ask for my life as payment for someone else's healing. He asks for my heart to remain yielded while my identity remains intact.

Jesus modeled this balance. He healed crowds but withdrew to lonely places to pray (Luke 5:16). He carried the cross, but He did not carry every demand placed upon Him by others. Obedience was His mission, but boundaries were His protection.

I once believed that obedience meant enduring anything without question. Now I understand that obedience also includes knowing when to step back so the burden does not become bondage.

### *Compassion vs. Responsibility*

Compassion is the willingness to care. Responsibility is the discernment of what is mine to hold onto.

I learned that I could show up for Red without becoming responsible for his emotional world. I could support him without allowing his suffering to interfere with my identity. Love does not require collapse. Caregiving does not require captivity.

In the past, when I confused responsibility with redemption, I became exhausted. When I surrendered responsibility back to God, my path became steadier, and inner peace became more attainable.

### *Therapeutic Lens*

From a psychological perspective, this healing work is also about nervous system stewardship. When we repeatedly bear emotional weight that does not belong to us, the body interprets it as a persistent threat. Over time, this leads to chronic stress, hypervigilance, fatigue, and emotional shutdown. Boundaries are not just spiritual wisdom; they are also a form of trauma-informed self-regulation. Each time you choose not to absorb what is not yours to carry, your body learns to feel safe again. Your breathing steadies. Your muscles release. Your mind regains clarity. Faith and physiology converge here: when you "cast your cares upon Him," your nervous system follows your obedience into a state of rest. This is why obedience with boundaries strengthens your ability to show compassion to yourself and others. You are no longer serving from depletion, but from a place of regulated peace, where love flows without self-erasure.

Trauma recovery teaches that reenactment of past events without boundaries leads to re-injury. Spiritually, the same truth holds: that obedience without emotional containment leads to soul fatigue.

In therapy, I learned to practice *empathic detachment*, which is to witness pain without merging with it. Spiritually, I learned to trust that God can carry what I cannot. Each boundary I voiced helped regulate my nervous system and prevented stress and anguish from piling up. Each moment I stepped away from verbal aggression helped me align with my best self. Obedience became sustainable when it stopped costing me my inner peace.

## *Case Study*

A ministry leader betrayed by a close friend wrestled for months in prayer. When he finally released it, he discovered deeper compassion and a stronger anointing to lead.

## *Tools and Practices*

### Spiritual Tools

- Write out your wrestle with God: "Lord, this is where it hurts… this is what I'm afraid of… this is what I don't understand." Notice how your language shifts over time from panic to trust; this is healing in motion.
- Breathe slowly as you sit with Psalm 34:18 when you feel broken, Matthew 11:28-30 when you feel overloaded, and Galatians 6:2-5 when you're confused about what is yours to

hold onto. Let the words guide both your nervous system and your choices.

- Share your story with one or two safe people who can listen without trying to fix. Having someone witness your struggle reduces shame and supports the regulation of your nervous system.

Therapeutic Practices

- When you feel emotionally flooded, place a hand on your chest and take 5 slow breaths, exhaling longer than you inhale to signal safety to your body.
- In a journal (or with a friend), rehearse phrases like, "If you speak to me that way, I will step out." Practicing calm language prepares your mind and body to use it.
- Ask yourself: "What am I feeling in my body? What is mine to carry right now?" Use the answer to choose either to stay present with compassion or to step away in peace.

### *Reflection and Action*

- What area of forgiveness feels like a wrestle right now?
- How is God reshaping your heart in the tension?
- How can I offer compassion without surrendering my peace?

Write down one responsibility you are releasing back to God today. What you release, He restores in right proportion.

### *Faith Declaration*

"I declare that my wrestle is not wasted. God is birthing resilience and blessing in my struggle. My compassion is strong, my boundaries are holy, and my peace is preserved by the wisdom of God."

*Faith Prayer*

"Lord, teach me how to obey You without abandoning myself. Give me the clarity to know what is mine to carry and the humility to release what belongs to You. Let my compassion be rooted in wisdom, my service be anchored in peace, and my obedience be guided by Your voice alone. Amen."

*Framework Truth*

Holy obedience is only bearing the burden that God places in your hands and returning the rest to Him. You can step back into challenging places and situations with compassion without surrendering your peace or your identity. Every boundary you honor breaks agreement with bondage. When you release what was never yours to hold, the weight you feared would crush you shifts to the shoulders of the One who promised to carry it, and you are finally free to love from a place of safety and rest.

*The Forgiveness Framework™ – Capacity*

In this season, we need to consider Capacity, or the understanding that forgiveness cannot move faster than a person's emotional and spiritual readiness. Wanting to forgive does not automatically mean someone has the internal resources to do so safely. Capacity grows through support, therapy, spiritual grounding, and nervous-system stability. It develops as we learn language for grief, anger, betrayal, and loss. Capacity protects us from self-abandonment and reminds us that God does not call us to forgiveness that re-wounds the soul. Instead, He meets us where we are and strengthens what has been weakened over time. Forgiveness without capacity becomes fragile and unsustainable; forgiveness rooted in capacity becomes steady, grounded, and life-giving. As capacity expands, the heart slowly gains strength to move forward without collapsing back into harm.

Framework 3

# The Call You Didn't Want

—✦—

***The "yes" you resist is often the doorway to the healing you've been praying for.***

When we hear the word sacrifice, we often imagine grand, singular acts; heroic moments that end in clear resolution. Rarely do we think of the quiet, continuous surrender that tests one's faith. Yet, it's this long-haul obedience, saying "yes" to God daily, that forges character and deepens trust.

For me, that prolonged "yes" stretched across eight grueling months in the hospital beside Red. There were no sudden breakthroughs or tidy endings; just the steady rhythm of care, prayer, and exhaustion. But in that season, God transformed obedience from duty into devotion. My "yes" became both my weapon and my witness.

During those long eight months, I learned the geography of the hospital like the back of my hand, from the neonatal unit to the hospice wing—a place where birth and death existed under one roof. Perspective came quickly in that environment. The trivial frustrations of daily life vanished beside the gravity of suffering and survival.

Caregiving demanded both physical stamina and emotional endurance. My back ached from nights spent in a recliner; my eyes stung from sleepless vigils. Stress-induced migraines became routine companions. Yet, amidst it all, I uttered short prayers in the elevator: "God, sustain me. God, use me." I discovered that obedience doesn't always feel holy; it often feels heavy. But within that weight, I found strength because I led me to lean even more on God.

## Spiritual Recalibration

Red's condition rose and fell like a storm tide with moments of improvement followed by sudden regression. The emotional whiplash was real. One day I would celebrate progress; the next I would hold my breath through another ICU crisis.

And then there were his moods. Pain made him volatile; fear made him cruel. There were days when his words reopened wounds I thought had healed. Yet even then, I heard the Spirit tell me, "Stay the course." Forgiveness wasn't a one-time decision; it was a daily discipline.

Most nights for me ended in the hospital chapel. There, beneath dim lights and the scent of candles, I learned to pray not for outcomes, but for alignment. At first, I prayed for rescue. Later, I prayed for revelation. My petitions shifted from "Change this" to "Change me." Slowly, my heart synchronized with heaven's pace.

There were nights when doubt sat beside me like an uninvited guest. And just when I considered stepping away, a nurse would mention how calm Red seemed when I was around, or I would read a verse that pierced the fog, like Luke 22:42, "Yet not my will, but Yours be done."

During this time, my mother and daughter became my anchors. They brought food, laughter, and reminders of life beyond hospital walls. Early on in my caregiving process with Red, on a particularly challenging day, Aniyah's simple words stopped me in my tracks: "Mom, maybe loving Dad like God loves us is part of your healing, too."

Red's vulnerability exposed the man behind the pride. During one difficult outburst, he shouted, "I never asked you to stay!" The words cut deep, but later, when he muttered, "I'm just scared," I could see the frightened humanity beneath the anger. That moment reminded me that obedience isn't about fixing someone; it's about being faithful to God's instruction.

## Lessons in Sacrificial Love

Before this, I thought sacrifice meant giving something up. But God redefined it: true sacrifice is the surrender of self. It's staying when leaving would feel easier. It's forgiving when forgetting feels safer.

Through prayer and wise counsel, I learned that love and boundaries coexist. Saying "yes" to God didn't mean saying "yes" to abuse or disrespect. Setting limits was not rebellion; it was stewardship. It protected both my peace and Red's dignity.

There were days when divine fingerprints became visible, like in a sudden improvement in lab results or a recovery that baffled doctors. Each small miracle said to me, "I see you. Keep saying yes."

## Witnessing ~~Red's~~ Our Transformation

By month six in the hospital, Red began saying "thank you" to me. He noticed my sacrifices and even asked how I was doing. It was subtle but significant. Gratitude became the first fruit of humility sprouting in his life.

Later, he confessed, "I took everything for granted—my health, you, our family." For the first time, the remorse from him felt real. When I replied simply, "I forgive you," it wasn't for him alone; it was for me, too.

Healing was happening in both Red and me. Those eight months peeled back my defenses, forcing me to confront fears and insecurities buried under years of hurt.

Therapy sessions with my counselor became sacred pauses in my day where I unpacked pain with truth and grace. God was refining me by building endurance, compassion, and a deeper understanding of His heart. My "yes" had turned into self-transformation. What started as obedience had become an invitation into purpose.

## The Fragile Edge of Hope

As Red's name climbed the transplant list, hope and fear intertwined into every corner of our lives. Every ring of my phone made my pulse quicken. *Would this be the call?*

Red's vulnerability deepened. "I don't want to die," he admitted.

My answer to that was simple: "God is not finished with you yet." Whether healing came through surgery or surrender, I trusted that obedience had already birthed something eternal within him and within me.

## The Harvest of Endurance

Galatians 6:9 declares, "Let us not become weary in doing good, for at the proper time we will reap a harvest if we do not give up." The harvest from this season in my life wasn't instant, but it was abundant. It showed up in peace where there used to be pain and in compassion where bitterness once ruled. Those eight months showed me that obedience to God's may not always glamorous, but it's always glorious. Saying "yes" to God, even when we don't want to, transforms suffering into sanctification.

## Spiritual Reflection

*Principle*

Forgiveness requires obedience. The wrestle prepares you, but the blessing comes when you say "yes."

*Scripture Anchors*

- "Yet not my will, but Yours be done." – Luke 22:42

- "If you are willing and obedient, you shall eat the good of the land." – Isaiah 1:19

## *Therapeutic Lens*

From a counseling perspective, obedience to God in seasons like this mirrors what therapists call *values-based resilience,* or the ability to endure hardship because meaning around the suffering or challenge is anchored to purpose. When a person acts in alignment with their deeply held values, such as faith, compassion, or integrity, the brain releases resilience-supporting chemicals that sustain emotional stamina over time. In simple terms, finding and developing one's purpose helps them to regulate their emotional pain. Without meaning, endurance leads to burnout, but with meaning, endurance becomes a method of refinement. Therapy also teaches that prolonged caregiving can activate grief, fear, and helplessness all at once, which is why emotional support and spiritual grounding are essential for our well-being. Obedience, when rooted in discernment and supported by healthy boundaries, protects the nervous system from collapse. Spiritually and psychologically, surrender is the steady decision to trust God with the outcome while consciously choosing alignment over escape.

Commitment to going to therapy and doing the inner work emphasizes the power of values-based action. Spiritually, obedience aligns us with God's healing process and His timing.

## *Tools and Practices*

### Spiritual Tools

- Each day, write one place you sensed God inviting a "yes," and one emotion you felt about it. Invite the Holy Spirit to show you where obedience is refining you, not exhausting you.
- Whether it's 12 a.m. or 12 p.m. in a parked car, dedicate a specific time to pray, "Not my will, but Yours," and release the outcome back to God.

- Speak verses like Luke 22:42, Galatians 6:9, and Isaiah 1:19 aloud, not as magic words but as agreements: "Lord, align my heart with this truth today."

Therapeutic Practices

- Practice slow, deep breaths (inhale 4, exhale 6) before entering or leaving a challenging or emotional place to signal safety to your nervous system.
- Schedule short, predictable breaks (a walk outside, a cup of tea, a quick stretch) to prevent compassion fatigue and emotional collapse. This is especially helpful for caregivers and those in helping professions.
- Ask, "Is this action aligned with my God-given values of faith, compassion, and wisdom?" This mirrors values-based resilience and keeps your "yes" from becoming self-erasure.

### *Case Study: The Pastor's "Yes"*

A pastor once wrestled deeply with betrayal from one of his closest ministry leaders. Though outwardly strong, he carried hidden resentment that began to drain his joy and dull his preaching. For months, he prayed for relief but refused to forgive, believing that the offender didn't deserve grace.

One night during prayer, he sensed the Holy Spirit utter, "Say 'yes' to Me." That simple instruction shattered his pride. Through tears, he forgave because God commanded him to release it. In the weeks that followed, his messages regained power, his congregation sensed renewed presence, and even his health began to improve.

His "yes" became a catalyst for healing, not only in his own heart but across his entire church. What began as obedience birthed revival.

Obedience opens the door to healing, but obedience also requires protection. The yes must now be safeguarded with boundaries that become holy.

### *Lesson*

Every "yes" to God—no matter how big or small—creates ripples of transformation far beyond what we can see.

### *Reflection and Action*

- Where is God asking for my "yes" today?
- What freedom might be released through my obedience?

### *Faith Declaration*

"I declare that my 'yes' unlocks Heaven's power. What I surrender, God redeems."

### *Faith Prayer*

"Lord, I yield my will to Yours. Give me strength to say 'yes,' even when I don't understand. Let my obedience open doors of healing for generations."

### *Framework Truth*

The call you didn't want from God is often the assignment that shapes you the most. Your obedient "yes," uttered through tears and fatigue, and upheld through faith, holds more spiritual force than any public victory ever could.

Sacrifice does not hollow you out; it refines you. What you lay down in surrender, God returns in sanctified strength.

Your obedience may feel costly now, but it is never wasted. Every prayer offered in exhaustion, every boundary set in wisdom, and every act of love extended when retreat seems easier becomes an eternal investment. The "yes" that breaks you open is the same "yes" God uses to build you whole. And when you look back one day, you will finally see what obedience created in you.

### *The Forgiveness Framework™ – Integration Begins*

This is the stage where forgiveness is no longer just an idea but begins to seep into behavior, decision-making, and spiritual posture. Integration allows the heart to hold the story without dissolving into shame or self-betrayal. It is the moment when forgiveness moves from spoken words to embodied truth; when boundaries are honored, emotions are acknowledged, and the soul refuses to return to old cycles. Integration means being able to engage the past without returning to bondage, to act with compassion without surrendering dignity, and to extend grace without losing identity. When forgiveness integrates, it becomes lived alignment, and the heart begins to walk with steadiness instead of survival.

Framework 4

# When Boundaries Become Holy

—✦—

***Forgiveness releases the past, but boundaries protect your future.***

To outsiders, my marriage to Red might have appeared ordinary at first. We were two people who fell in love, exchanged vows with joy, and built what looked like a promising life together. But beneath the surface, there existed a hidden labyrinth of emotional abuse, manipulation, and spiritual distortion. It was a relationship that both shaped and shattered me. It became a crucible where my understanding of love, grace, and obedience was tested beyond what I thought I could endure.

Sharing this is not about vilifying Red or seeking sympathy. It is about truth-telling and spiritual clarity, understanding how easily love can be entangled with pain when boundaries are absent, and how even in the ashes of brokenness, God's grace can still birth healing. What once broke me down became the soil where I learned to grow a different kind of love rooted in alignment with God.

## The Beginning

From the start, Red impressed me with his self-assuredness. He was focused, driven, and spoke with conviction about his goals. He was charming in a way that drew others in…and I was no exception. He surprised me with flowers at work, left handwritten notes in my purse, and spoke words that made me feel seen. Those early days felt intoxicating.

Looking back, I can now see the pattern for what it was: love-bombing, a shower of affection that built up my dependency on him. His praise became the air I breathed, and his approval became my compass. Whenever he offered small criticisms, I brushed them off, reasoning, "He's just being honest." What I didn't realize was that I was slowly surrendering my sense of self for the illusion of stability.

Still, there were subtle moments when something inside me screamed, "This doesn't feel right." He belittled people he deemed "too emotional" or "weak." He mocked a friend I deeply respected, calling her "too dramatic." I told myself he just didn't understand her personality. But that pit in my stomach was discernment, God's voice, trying to warn me that confidence without humility often becomes a platform for controlling behavior.

Yet I ignored the signs. My love for Red and my hope for marriage made me minimize behaviors that would later become full-grown patterns of manipulation. Denial became my coping mechanism; peace became my performance.

## The Gradual Shift Toward Control

Our wedding was beautiful, filled with laughter, tears, and sacred vows before God. But shortly after our honeymoon, the shift began. Red started taking control of our finances, insisting it was "more efficient." He began policing my wardrobe, saying, "That skirt is too short for a married woman." His tone was wrapped in care, but his intent was about control.

At first, I mistook his possessiveness for protection. I wanted to believe he loved me deeply. But soon, his "advice" became demands, and his opinions became law. I began to feel smaller in my own home.

Red's words often came with a double edge: "You're so smart, but you could be smarter if you just listened more." Or, "I'm just helping you improve." These constant corrections eroded my self-esteem until I questioned my worth and my sanity.

Friends noticed, too. They would ask, "Are you okay? You don't seem like yourself lately." I would smile and deflect. "We're fine; it's just normal marriage stuff." But inside, I felt like I was disappearing. My laughter was replaced with silence and my confidence replaced by caution. I learned to measure every word to avoid the sting of his criticism or disappointment.

Because we were Christians, church life was woven into our routine. Red often quoted Scripture, but selectively. He would emphasize Ephesians 5:22: "Wives, submit yourselves to your own husbands," yet conveniently omitted verse 25 of the same chapter: "Husbands, love your wives as Christ loved the church." His tone made it sound as though obedience to him equaled obedience to God.

The Bible, which had always been my source of comfort, became a weapon turned against me. He would accuse me of spiritual rebellion when I tried to express hurt. "You're being disobedient," he would say. "A godly wife knows her place." So, I began to equate silence with holiness and submission with safety. But deep down, I knew God's heart was not abusive. Still, fear made me quiet.

Red disliked community accountability. He avoided small groups or Bible studies that encouraged openness. "We don't need outsiders meddling in our business," he would say. Gradually, I became isolated from those who could speak truth into my situation. Even at church, we appeared as a perfect couple, smiling, serving, and participating. But behind closed doors, I was shrinking beneath the weight of spiritual manipulation.

Isolation is the breeding ground of control. Without wise counsel, I doubted my own discernment. Even my prayers became hesitant, as if God's voice had been drowned out by Red's demands.

## The Winter of Awakening

The breaking point came one cold evening when Red accused me of flirting with a male colleague. His jealousy erupted into a torrent of cruel words. I tried to explain, but he would not listen; his rage filled the room. He slammed doors, shouted accusations, and left me trembling on the kitchen floor.

That night, something inside me changed. Amid my tears, I heard a whisper deep within my spirit: "This is not love." For the first time, I allowed myself to see the truth. My marriage had become a prison disguised as devotion.

In the weeks that followed, I began planning. I sought out a Christian counselor trained in trauma recovery. She told me something that changed my life: "Preserving your peace is not rebellion; it is obedience to the God who made you." Her words broke the chains of false guilt I had carried.

I began researching legal options and women's shelters. I met discreetly with a trusted friend who promised safety if I needed to leave. Every plan I made was a step of faith. Fear followed me, but so did grace. For the first time in years, I began to feel God's voice again—not in condemnation, but in rescue.

## The Aftermath of Leaving

When I finally left, Red alternated between fury and tears, along with manipulation and pleading. He promised change, quoted Scripture about forgiveness, and accused me of "destroying our covenant." But my decision was final. I packed two suitcases, held my friend's hand, who comforted me during that time, and drove away with tears streaming down my face. I was not running from my marriage or "marriage" in general; I was running *toward* survival.

The process of going through a divorce was agonizing. Red fought to maintain control even from afar through messages, through mutual friends, and through guilt. He quoted verses about reconciliation, twisting them into what felt like spiritual chains. Yet I held onto the truth my counselor had helped me uncover: Forgiveness does not require proximity. I could forgive him without being emotionally or physically close to him. The wise words of a counselor, not to mention God's Word, insisted that I try. The seeds were planted, even if I wasn't ready to water them just yet.

I wrestled with guilt, sleepless nights, and the haunting question, "Did I fail God?" Healing came slowly, through trauma therapy, prayer, and community. Scripture became my medicine, especially Proverbs 4:23—"Guard your heart above all else, for it determines the course of your life." God was teaching me to guard my heart and not to harden it. I could still let the love of others enter into my life without putting my walls up due to past heartache with Red.

Months later, healing began to bloom like spring after a long winter. I volunteered at a women's shelter, sharing my story with others trapped in similar cycles. I discovered that vulnerability became my ministry. I prayed, "Lord, use these scars," and He did. My pain became a platform for compassion for others.

## Rewriting the Narrative

Years later, when Red's health began to decline, the seeds of forgiveness planted by my counselor while going through divorce began to bloom. I could care for him without losing myself. This was grace, but a guarded version of it. I had forgiven him long before this call, but forgiveness in action did not mean I was going to reenter past toxicity. Instead, I sought God's will carefully, ensuring that my obedience to His will by taking care of Red was rooted in peace.

During this time, I learned that healing is not a straight line; it is a spiral of layers, each one requiring renewed grace. While going through the divorce proceedings, there were days I felt strong, and days I felt fragile. There were moments when old triggers resurfaced and others when peace filled every corner of my heart.

My therapist once told me, "Forgiveness releases the offense; boundaries protect the healed version of you." Those words have become an anchor for me. I realized that love without limits is not love; it is enablement. Grace without structure leads to burnout. God was teaching me that boundaries are not barriers to compassion; they are bridges to peace.

## Spiritual Reflection

### *Statement of Truth*

When grace matures, it gains structure. I realize that love must have limits and that grace without boundaries becomes burnout. Here, I'm learning the divine language of no:

- No to manipulation.
- No to emotional debt.
- No to the false guilt that made me overextend.

Boundaries do not shrink my love; they secure it. Protecting my peace is not selfish; it is stewardship.

### *Principle*

Forgiveness is obedience, but boundaries are wisdom. Boundaries protect your healing and prevent repeated wounding. They are not walls of bitterness—they are guardrails of grace.

Even Jesus had boundaries. He withdrew to pray, He chose twelve disciples, and He did not entrust Himself to everyone (John 2:24).

I once thought forgiving Red meant giving him full access to me and my emotional life again. But God showed me that restoration looks different when safety and stewardship are involved. Forgiveness can coexist with distance. Grace can be firm and gentle at the same time.

## *Forgiveness vs. Reconciliation*

Forgiveness is unconditional but reconciliation requires trust. Forgiveness releases the offender from emotional debt. Reconciliation rebuilds the relationship, which requires evidence of change. I learned the hard way that reconnection without repentance becomes a revolving door of pain.

When Red sought forgiveness, I gave it freely. But I also held firm to the boundaries that protected my peace. This distinction allowed me to walk in grace without returning to bondage.

## *Therapeutic Lens*

Trauma-informed care shows that setting boundaries are essential for preventing re-traumatization. Spiritually, setting boundaries align with Proverbs 4:23: "Guard your heart above all else, for it determines the course of your life."

From a counseling perspective, establishing boundaries is also a form of nervous system protection. When someone has lived under chronic control, criticism, or manipulation, the body learns to stay hyper-alert, constantly scanning for threats. Without boundaries, the nervous system never fully resets; it remains stuck in defense mode. Boundaries signal safety to the brain and body. They teach the heart, "I am allowed to stop. I am allowed to choose peace." This is why many people feel guilt when they first begin setting limits, because the body is not used to safety yet. But over time, healthy boundaries restore internal order. Spiritually, this mirrors God's design for rest, Sabbath, and refuge. Boundaries are not emotional walls; they are sacred invitations back into calm, clarity, and self-respect under God's covering.

In therapy, I learned to map my triggers, name my limits, and trust my intuition. Spiritually, I learned to let the Holy Spirit be my counselor, reminding me that saying "no" is sometimes the holiest answer I can give someone.

Boundaries became my way of worship as an act of honoring what God healed in me.

### *Case Study*

A pastor once forgave a former staff member who had betrayed him. Though he extended grace, he chose not to rehire the individual. That boundary allowed forgiveness to flow while protecting the integrity of the ministry. In the aftermath, the church didn't crumble; it grew healthier.

This reminded me of my own journey with Red. Forgiveness restored my soul, but boundaries protected my future. Both can coexist without contradiction.

### *Tools and Practices*

#### Spiritual Tools

- Sit with Proverbs 4:23 and Matthew 10:14. Ask, "What does guarding my heart look like in this situation? And "Where is Jesus inviting me to 'shake the dust off' and move on in peace?" Let these verses guide where access needs to tighten and where you can release guilt.
- Write down a list of people you have forgiven. Next to each name, note: *Level of access (high / medium / low)* and *Impact on my peace (nurturing / neutral / draining)*. Pray over each name and ask, "Lord, what level of access is wise in this season?"
- Ask the Holy Spirit, "Show me one line I need to draw to protect what You've healed." Then pray for courage to keep that line when it's tested.

#### Therapeutic Practices

- Grounding and Breath: When you feel pressured or controlled, pause, place a hand on your chest, and pray, "Lord, guard my heart."

- Boundary Scripts: Write and practice simple phrases like, "I'm not available for that," or "I need to stop this conversation now."
- Support Check-In: Regularly process boundary decisions with a trusted friend, mentor, or therapist who honors both your faith and your safety.

## *Reflection and Action*

- Where do I need to establish boundaries to protect my obedience?
- How can I honor God with both forgiveness and wisdom?
- In what relationships do I need to redefine access while maintaining compassion?

Write down one area where God is teaching you to say "no." Know that saying "no" to any and every dysfunction is a "yes" to a healthier and more purposeful life.

## *Faith Declaration*

"I declare my boundaries are blessed. What I forgive, God redeems; what I guard, God sustains. My grace is guarded, my peace is sacred, and my heart is secure in God's hands."

## *Faith Prayer*

"Lord, thank You for teaching me that forgiveness and wisdom are not opposites but allies. Give me the courage to love without losing myself, to forgive without forgetting wisdom, and to draw boundaries that bless, not block. May my guarded grace become a testimony of Your healing power. Amen."

## *Framework Truth*

Holy boundaries are where grace grows roots. They are the sacred lines that say, "I forgive you, but I will not abandon the healing God has done in me." Saying no to manipulation, emotional debt, and false guilt is not a lack of love; it is love that has learned wisdom. Guarding your heart is not running away from people; it is walking in step with God. When your forgiveness is covered by healthy boundaries, your peace becomes protected, your purpose becomes clearer, and your life becomes a safer place for God's love to dwell.

*The Forgiveness Framework™ – Release Without Re-Entry*

Release is the removal of emotional authority from the person or event that once held power over the heart. Release is not reconciliation, return, or renewed access. It does not dismiss consequences or diminish accountability. Rather, release marks the moment when the soul chooses freedom over bitterness, peace over rumination, and identity over entanglement. Release allows us to acknowledge what happened without allowing it to dictate who we are becoming. It honors boundaries as sacred and not selfish. In God's wisdom, release becomes a form of spiritual alignment; letting go of control while guarding the heart. Forgiveness expressed as release does not rebuild unsafe connections; it restores internal sovereignty and entrusts justice back into God's hands.

Framework 5

# When Letting Go Sets You Free

—✦—

***Freedom begins when you stop holding onto what God never required of you.***

Finally letting go of the emotional IOUs that had quietly accumulated over years of disappointment, betrayal, and unmet expectations was my moment of surrender. Doing so wasn't about forgetting the offense—far from it. It was more so about releasing the debt. Forgiveness never meant pretending that the pain didn't happen, which is incredibly unhealthy. True forgiveness means deciding not to let past pain become my permanent address.

I found freedom in the release when I discovered that bitterness and resentment are painful and heavy, and carrying these burdens for long periods of time prevents inner peace and costs more energy than healing ever will. Through this stage of healing, I learned how to care without trying to bear the load for them, how to love without losing myself inside that love, and how to extend compassion without enabling past harmful behavior.

Dropping the baggage full of emotional IOUs didn't happen overnight. It came in waves, sometimes in moments when I would think I was completely healed, only to realize there were still fragments of anger tucked away in hidden corners of my heart. Healing required honesty. I had to face not just what Red did to me, but what I had allowed myself to endure out of misplaced loyalty and distorted love.

## Beneath the Mask

Narcissism is more than self-admiration or arrogance; it's a survival system built on control, manipulation, and the relentless need to dominate the emotional atmosphere. In my years with Red, I studied that system firsthand because it was how Red operated. At the time, I didn't have a name for it and I didn't fully understand it. I only knew that something sacred inside me was constantly being diminished.

Red's personality could be magnetic; he was charming, eloquent, and persuasive. But behind the charisma lurked a subtle cruelty, a way of twisting words until I questioned my own reality. For a long time, I thought that if I prayed harder, loved deeper, and submitted more, things with him would change. I mistook endurance for obedience. I thought putting up with his dysfunction was my cross to bear. But God began to show me that faith does not require bondage, and love does not demand the death of one's identity.

The pattern of narcissism with Red always began the same way. First came the adoration with the kind of attention that sweeps you off your feet and makes you feel seen in bold technicolor. Red was a master at that. He wrote love letters filled with promises, planned spontaneous getaways, and seemed to understand my every need. In hindsight, he was love-bombing me as a strategic way to secure my devotion before the true power struggle began.

Not long after the compliments and showering of "love," did Red show his true colors. The compliments turned into criticisms, the laughter into sarcasm, and the warmth into calculated coldness. He began to question my judgment, mock my ideas, and subtly chip away at my confidence. It wasn't always loud or overt. Sometimes it was as simple as a sigh, an eyeroll, or a backhanded compliment that left me spinning.

I didn't realize it then, but I was being conditioned to seek validation from the person who was undermining me.

The gaslighting came next, which is how Red would rewrite reality. He would tell me certain things happened that I knew didn't or would insist that I had agreed to something I knew I hadn't. Over time, I started doubting my memory, my intuition, and even my sanity. It is a terrifying thing to lose trust in your own intuition and perception. You begin to outsource "truth" to the person who is most invested in keeping you disoriented—the narcissist.

And then came the isolation. Red would frame it as love: "I just want you to myself," or "They don't really care about you like I do." Slowly, I pulled away from friends and family, thinking I was protecting the relationship. In reality, I was cutting off my support system, giving him full access to my emotions without any accountability.

The most confusing part was the spiritual manipulation. Red knew Scripture, and he used it like a sword to cut through me rather than as a blanket or medicine to help comfort and encourage me. He would quote verses about submission, forgiveness, and loyalty to reinforce his control, while ignoring the parts about mutual respect, sacrificial love, and humility. It took me years to realize that any theology that demands you silence your voice is not Biblical—it is simply bondage dressed up as religion.

## Breaking the Chains

The first step to breaking free was naming what I had been living through. Without language, you live in confusion. Once I saw the pattern, I could finally begin to dismantle it. It wasn't just psychological clarity; it was spiritual revelation. The enemy thrives in secrecy, but truth is light, and the enemy can't thrive on truth or light.

I devoured every resource I could find—books, sermons, counseling sessions—anything that helped me understand what had been occurring in my marriage. With each new piece of knowledge, I felt God reclaiming territory in my mind. I began to pray differently, not as a woman begging for her marriage to be fixed, but as a daughter reclaiming her authority.

During that season of divorcing Red, I remember praying one day, "God, I refuse to believe lies about who I am. I am not crazy. I am not too much. I am not impossible to love." That prayer became one of my guiding lights. Slowly but surely, my spirit started to detox from years of manipulation. The real test came years later when God brought me back into Red's orbit when he was sick and in the hospital. He was weakened and vulnerable, but the old patterns still peeked through occasionally. Only now, I wasn't the same woman. I had learned how to show grace without surrendering my peace.

## The Return Encounter

Walking into Red's hospital room for the first time felt surreal. There he was, the man who once controlled the atmosphere of our home like an autocrat, now confined to a hospital bed, dependent on others for everything. It was humbling to witness. His words were softer, but I could still sense the urge to dominate in subtle ways, like complaining about the nurses or dictating small details just to feel powerful.

But this time, I knew how to engage with Red as a grounded woman with clear boundaries. "If you insult me or the nurses," I told him gently, "I will step out of the room." The first time I said it, he looked shocked, like he didn't recognize this version of me. But I wasn't angry or emotional. I was calm, kind, and firm. And that was new territory for both of us.

When he tried to argue about things that didn't happen, one time claiming I hadn't visited the day before, I simply said, "You may not remember, but I was here." I didn't defend, debate, or try to explain myself. I released the need to be believed. That, too, was part of dropping the baggage of past emotional hurt.

Empathy without enabling became my new practice. “I understand you’re afraid,” I would tell him, “but I won’t allow you to talk to me disrespectfully.” Compassion with boundaries is one of the highest forms of love. It allows mercy to flow without opening the door to manipulation.

## Spiritual Warfare and Inner Peace

Forgiveness is a spiritual discipline, but it’s also a strategy for survival. I began praying not just for protection from Red’s behavior, but for freedom from the emotional hooks that once kept me tethered to him. Scripture talks about binding and loosing; binding the forces that keep us trapped in unhealthy cycles and loosing the freedom that comes through truth.

There were nights I would leave the hospital and pray, “God, I bind every manipulative spirit at work in this situation, and I release Your peace into my heart.” That prayer wasn’t about controlling Red; it was only about reclaiming my spiritual atmosphere.

The paradox of forgiveness is that God will sometimes call you to intercede for the very person who caused your deepest pain, which is what happened with me. I began to pray for Red’s heart. Not for reconciliation, but for redemption. I asked God to dismantle the pride that kept him from seeing himself clearly. I didn’t know if those prayers would change him—but they certainly helped change me.

Toward the end of his hospital stay, Red started expressing regret. “I should have treated you better,” he said one night, his voice barely above a whisper. I wanted to believe it, but I had learned to look beyond words. True repentance shows up in consistent action. So, I watched. Did he take responsibility without shifting blame? Did he show respect to the nurses when no one was watching? I noticed subtle shifts, like in a softened tone of voice and fewer outbursts. Sure, they were small, almost imperceptible moments, but they were signs that the hardness within him was cracking.

Whether his transformation was lasting or temporary wasn't my responsibility to measure. My role was to stay in peace, to love in truth, and to finish the assignment God gave me, which was to show compassion without surrendering discernment.

## Mercy or Foolishness?

When people heard that I was caring for Red again, the reactions were mixed. Some applauded the grace I was showing him, while others thought I had lost my mind. "Why would you go back?" they asked. Their concern came from a place of love, but they didn't understand that obedience to God and reconciliation with an emotionally abusive ex-spouse are not the same thing.

I wasn't reconciling or returning to an old role; I was walking in a new revelation. I had no illusions of rekindling romance or erasing history. I was there because God asked me to extend mercy—but on His terms and not Red's.

There is a fine line between mercy and foolishness. Mercy extends a hand without compromising safety. Foolishness ignores red flags and calls it faith. I learned that mercy can say "yes" to compassion while saying "no" to toxicity.

## From Victim to Victor

Once you understand manipulation, you stop being its victim. Awareness dismantles control. Every time Red tried one of his old tactics, I stayed calm. When I didn't react, the old pattern broke. It was almost disorienting for him to see me rooted in strength and conviction. He didn't know how to handle the absence of chaos between the two of us. My peace disrupted his need for dominance. That is when I realized that peace is power. The enemy thrives on reaction, but peace silences his authority.

In those early days spent at the hospital, I saw something I had never seen before: a proud man stripped of pretense. The illness had taken his strength, and for the first time, I could see the fear behind his anger. Control had been his armor, but now that self-protection was gone. Beneath it was a wounded soul who never learned how to feel safe without grasping at control.

Seeing him that way didn't excuse what he had done, but it helped me understand what brokenness can do when left unhealed. And in that understanding, I found a sense of liberation.

## Hope in the Midst of Complexity

Forgiveness is rarely clean or simple. It's layered, cyclical, and sometimes messy. Some days, I felt empowered, while other days, waves of grief would wash over me from past emotional wounds inflicted by Red. But each time I chose to release resentment, I found that I was able to reclaim a little more of myself.

This stage of my journey—dropping the emotional baggage—was never about erasing the past; it was about extracting the wisdom from it. I learned that healing is not forgetting what happened, but remembering it without reliving it.

Through Red, I learned what love without wisdom costs. Through God, I learned that wisdom without love is empty and unfulfilling. The tension between those two truths became a place where grace and accountability coexist.

I don't know if Red ever experienced the full transformation I prayed for. What I do know is that God transformed me. I no longer hold onto the bitterness that once defined me. I can speak his name without flinching, recall our story without resentment, and thank God for what it taught me about boundaries, self-worth, and mercy.

Forgiveness does not rewrite history—it redeems it. It turns pain into testimony. And it reminds you that nothing, not even betrayal, can stop the purpose of God in your life.

So if you find yourself standing at your own crossroads of release, know that you are not called to carry what God has already redeemed. Drop the emotional baggage. Let peace into your life. The freedom you're afraid of losing is the very thing waiting on the other side of your surrender.

## Spiritual Reflection

### *Statement of Truth*

Letting go is not weakness; it is spiritual warfare. I am learning that forgiveness is not a feeling but a decision, and peace is not passive; it is powerful. I release:

- The debt I was never meant to collect.
- The resentment that once guarded my pain.
- The emotional weight of stories that no longer define me.

Forgiveness does not erase what happened. It breaks what once held me hostage. Releasing emotional IOUs is not denying injustice; it is refusing to be imprisoned by it. My freedom does not require their apology; it requires my obedience to peace.

### *Principle*

Forgiveness is a form of spiritual authority. When I forgive, I am not approving the harm; I am reclaiming my heart. Jesus taught that bitterness defiles the soul (Mark 7:20-23), and Paul warned that unforgiveness gives the enemy a foothold (Ephesians 4:27). Forgiveness interrupts spiritual access to my pain. This means that letting go is not losing; it is choosing not to be ruled by what wounded me.

### *Forgiveness vs. Emotional Entanglement*

Forgiveness releases the person. Emotional entanglement keeps the offense alive. I once believed that forgiving meant staying emotionally tied to the very behavior that harmed me. God showed me the difference. I can forgive without revisiting the injury. I can love without reentering dysfunction. Forgiveness closes the ledger. Entanglement keeps it open. Peace only multiplies where the account has been settled.

## *Therapeutic Lens*

From a therapeutic perspective, letting go often involves "grief work." You are not only grieving or releasing what happened; you are also releasing the future you thought you would have. Counselors call this *ambiguous loss,* which involves mourning something that is gone, even when the person or situation is still present in some form. Naming that grief in prayer to God prevents you from minimizing your pain or shaming yourself for "still feeling it." Grieving takes time, there's no hurrying through it, and the process and time frame is a little different for everyone, depending on the circumstances and the person's background.

Clinically, forgiveness also means interrupting old patterns of thinking: "I must stay angry to stay safe," or "If I forgive, it means what they did was acceptable." In counseling, we challenge these beliefs and replace them with truth. Spiritually, the Holy Spirit partners with that work, renewing the mind and anchoring the heart. Over time, your body begins to trust that you can remember the story without reliving the threat.

Trauma recovery teaches that unresolved resentment keeps the nervous system locked in survival mode. Spiritually, forgiveness resets from that place. When I released the offense, my body followed suit. My nervous system learned how to rest again. My spirit recognized safety.

In prayer, I learned to name what I was releasing: betrayal, humiliation, abandonment, control, and grief. Each name or phrase spoken aloud broke its hold on me. Forgiveness became an act of both neurological and spiritual healing. Letting go was not forgetting; it was finishing the fight.

## *Case Study*

A woman held anger toward her estranged father for over twenty years. She forgave him privately when his health declined, though they never reconciled. When he passed, she expected regret, but instead she experienced peace. The apology she never received no longer drained her emotional freedom. Her forgiveness did not restore the relationship. It restored her.

## *Tools and Practices*

### Spiritual Tools

- Sit with Colossians 3:13, Matthew 18:21-22, and Romans 12:19. Ask: *What debt am I still trying to collect? Where am I holding onto revenge or control?* Let these verses gently reorient your heart toward release, not denial.
- List what you believe you are owed (apologies, explanations, accountability, validation). Next to each one, prayerfully write: "I release this debt into God's hands." Notice what feels hardest to release and talk honestly with God about it.
- Speak the person's name before God. Name the harm specifically. Then pray: "Lord, I release this debt. Cleanse what remains in me." Repeat as often as needed; forgiveness is a process and not a single moment.

### Therapeutic Practices

- Write the story of what happened from your perspective, then add a second paragraph titled "What I am learning." This honors grief while extracting wisdom.
- On paper, practice simple boundary statements: "I won't stay in this conversation if it becomes disrespectful," and "This 'no' is final and I need you to honor that." Use them as scripts when you feel pulled back into old patterns.

- Choose one safe, wise person (friend, pastor, counselor) and share one "emotional IOU" you're working to release. Being heard in a safe space reinforces both healing and letting go.

### *Reflection and Action*

- What emotional debt am I still collecting?
- Where has bitterness disguised itself as protection?
- What would change in my life if I released this offense today?

Write down one name, one memory, and/or one wound you are ready to release. This is not for their sake, but for your own healing.

### *Faith Declaration*

"I release what tried to bind me. I forgive without returning to bondage. I choose peace over resentment, truth over bitterness, and freedom over fear. What once wounded me no longer rules me. I am healed enough to let go."

### *Faith Prayer*

"Lord, I surrender every emotional debt I have been carrying. I lay down what You never asked me to hold onto. Teach me to forgive as You forgive; not to excuse the harm, but to release its power over me. Restore my peace, renew my mind, and let the freedom of forgiveness finish its work in my life. Amen."

### *Framework Truth*

Letting go is an act of courage that ends your agreement with bondage. Forgiveness releases the emotional IOUs you were never meant to hold onto and places every account in God's hands. When you stop rehearsing old injuries, your heart begins to breathe again, and peace finds a home inside you. Healthy boundaries then grow strong around that peace, allowing you to love with clarity instead of fear. In choosing to release the debt, you step out of victimhood and into spiritual authority; the past no longer rules you, and your freedom becomes proof that God has been at work in your story.

*The Forgiveness Framework™ – Release as Healing*

In this chapter, The Forgiveness Framework deepens into a maturing expression of Release, which is a gentle loosening of the cords that once bound the heart in resentment, fear, or emotional debt. It is learning to remember without reliving and to care without being consumed. Release honors grief, acknowledges impact, and still chooses peace. It represents the shift from emotional entanglement to spiritual stability, from holding onto the weight of another person's choices to reclaiming one's inner ground. This form of forgiveness allows the soul to exhale and rest in God's protection. Release becomes a declaration: "This no longer has authority over me." And in that surrender, freedom gradually unfolds.

Framework 6

# When Healing Changes Your Name

— ✦ —

***You are not what happened to you but who you chose to become after it.***

After release came revelation. I began to see my story differently. What once looked like failure began to look like God forming something purposeful in my life. This was where my healing turned into meaning.

Through redemptive reframing of the divorce with Red and all the past hurts from that relationship, I stopped asking, "Why did this happen?" and started asking, "What can this teach me?" I learned that finding purpose doesn't come from avoiding pain; it comes from understanding it. I began to realize that my past didn't disqualify me from ministry and service and a relationship with God; it qualified me.

Looking back in hindsight can be profoundly holy if we choose it to be. It is where broken pieces begin to make sense, not because the pain we went through was justified, but because it was used for a greater good. It is the divine economy of grace: nothing is wasted and everything is redeemed. What a beautiful promise God offers, but only if we allow that promise into our lives.

## Seeing Through New Eyes

When forgiveness truly settles in the soul, perspective changes. What used to be triggers can become teachers. The moments that once replayed as torment begin to play back as testimony to what you've been through and how God is still working in your life. You stop rehearsing past pain and start recognizing the patterns that once (or twice) led you there. You begin to notice that every betrayal taught you discernment, every disappointment taught you detachment from the one who did you harm, and every moment filled with tears and prayer taught you dependence on God.

In those evenings after Red's treatments, I would sometimes sit in the hospital parking lot watching the sun dip below the horizon, tucking itself in for the night. The air always seemed heavier at the hospital, thick with stories of survival, loss, and fragile hope. But on those particular days when I would watch the sun set, I felt a strange sense of peace. I was no longer rushing to make sense of everything. I was letting it make sense to me, in its own time. Sometimes, God uses the wonder of nature to help the mind and the nervous system slow down to make way for mental clarity.

Healing had rearranged my sightline. What once looked like punishment—a past divorce and a present filled with a broken man I thought I had said goodbye to forever—began to look like preparation for a transformation in my life. The very circumstances that felt like God's rejection were actually His redirection. I began to understand that closure wasn't the end of something painful; it was the beginning of something sacred.

## Redemptive Reframing: The Turning Point

Redemptive reframing does not mean I had to pretend that the pain from my past marriage with Red didn't happen; it means I had to position the pain differently. Instead of sitting inside my wounds, I started standing on them—owning them, listening to what they had to teach, and not shying away from them. They became platforms, elevated spaces of wisdom where empathy, strength, and vision could grow.

I used to think healing meant trying to erase your past; it seemed like a logical part of the process. Except, now I know that healing means acceptance that it happened, but under the lens of "I get to choose what kind of story I want to tell." Sure, the pain and the wounds happened, and at the same time, I get to choose the lessons I learned as a result and how I'm going to use those past experiences to help others—all while maintaining my dependence on God. Redemptive reframing is what happens when you hand your pain back to God and ask Him to narrate it again, this time through the lens of purpose.

In the hospital, each time Red and I interacted, I could feel redemptive reframing happening in real-time. There were still tender spots, moments where I felt the tug of old emotions—the ache of what was or the grief for what would never be—but they no longer dictated my response. They simply reminded me that I was human, healing, and held by the Almighty.

Initially, I had prayed for release, but what I received was revelation. Initially, I had asked for answers, but what I received was understanding. That is the essence of reframing: you don't need to rewrite the past; you just need to reread it with healed eyes.

## Surprising Conversations with Red

Despite the boundaries, Red and I found moments of surprising candor. One afternoon, while adjusting his pillows, he asked with a gentle voice, "Do you ever regret helping me?"

The question caught me off guard. For a moment, I flashed back to the day I fled our house, then returned to more recent emotions of the anxiety of returning to his life for the sake of his medical care and the rollercoaster of anger and compassion since then. So many versions of me had existed in this story: the wife, the caregiver, and the woman trying to move forward with her life yet drawn back by grace.

But the answer that rose in my heart was simple and true. "No, I don't regret it," I told him. "There are days when it's hard, but I think this is where God wanted me to be. For both of us."

He nodded with tears forming at the corners of his eyes, and simply said, "Thank you."

That brief exchange, though sparse in words, held great significance in that there was mutual acknowledgment between the two of us. It was as if we both recognized how caring for him had led me to an unexpected gift of my own closure. For so long, I had believed closure would come through distance or finality. But it came through service. It came through compassion. It came through God using the same space that once wounded me as the soil where forgiveness would grow.

Still, I didn't interpret those moments as an invitation to revert to old intimacy. If anything, they were signposts of something new—a relationship that might eventually settle into co-parenting friendship or remain a gentle companionship marked by shared history and faith. I didn't know, and surprisingly, I was okay with the uncertainty. That acceptance was proof of how far I had come.

## From Pain to Perspective

There is a phrase that often echoes in therapy rooms and sacred spaces alike: "Pain that is not transformed is transmitted." That truth became real to me in those months. Every time I resisted bitterness, I was transforming pain. Every time I chose compassion over resentment, I was rewiring emotional patterns that had been generations deep.

Reframing didn't happen overnight. It came in layers—slow, steady, sometimes subtle. It came through journaling late at night, through small prayers uttered in the hospital hallway, and through laughter that surfaced unexpectedly in between doctors' rounds. It came in the way I could finally talk about Red without tension tightening my chest. It came in being able to say, "He hurt me," and also, "He was hurting." The ability to balance holding truth and tenderness together felt incredibly liberating. I was no longer beholden to my emotions regarding my past with Red—and they would no longer color the present moment.

I started noticing that my conversations with others shifted, too. I could listen to their pain without immediately jumping into "fix-it mode." I had learned to honor the simplicity in being present for someone. I had learned that transformation is less about information and more about revelation, seeing with spiritual sight what once looked senseless.

Through redemptive reframing, my empathy for others and myself deepened. My leadership skills sharpened. Trust in others and self-trust returned. I began to believe that I could discern without being defensive, that I could love without losing myself, and that I could show compassion without surrendering healthy boundaries. Maturity in healing looks like loving wisely, which is what I began to do.

## Spiritual Reflection

The pain you avoid may be able to provide you the wisdom you need. It's not the event that destroys us; it's the meaning we attach to it. When we choose a different meaning, our energy changes, too. Pain, when reframed, becomes a portal to finding purpose.

### *Forgiveness Doesn't Erase Memory; It Redeems It*

Memories of past hurts used to sting. But now they share a testimony. Every recollection that once triggered tears now reminds me of triumph. I didn't forget; I forgave. And in forgiving, I reframed my past and used it to help find my purpose.

### *Boundaries Can Breathe*

Healing helped me see that boundaries aren't barriers; they're breathing spaces. They keep relationships from suffocating under the weight of unrealistic expectations. I learned to build boundaries with love and maintain them over time with peace.

### *Grace Can Coexist with Grief*

You can be grateful for the growth and still grieve the loss. Healing does not mean pretending the hurt never happened; it means it no longer holds you hostage.

### *Perspective Produces Peace*

The reframed mind doesn't need every answer; it rests in understanding that even the hard things serve a holy purpose.

### *A Shift in Identity*

Redemptive reframing not only changed how I viewed Red; it changed how I viewed myself. For years, I wore labels born out of circumstance like, betrayed wife, single mother, and overcomer. Each label held the residue of expectations, limitations, and unspoken burdens. But through healing, I rediscovered my true identity: chosen, whole, and evolving. I was no longer defined by what I endured but by what I embodied.

The reframed woman is not naive. She doesn't romanticize redemption. She recognizes the cost. She understands that sometimes, the miracle is not in resurrection but in resurrection power: getting up again, wiser and softer at the same time.

That realization reshaped how I approached leadership. My voice grew steadier. My compassion deepened. My confidence no longer came from proving how strong I was; it came from resting in peace.

The lessons that came through Red's illness and our shared journey changed my heart and recalibrated my calling. They birthed frameworks, coaching models, and faith-based curricula that now help others navigate their own healing. That's the divine multiplier effect of reframing; when your private healing becomes someone else's public cry for help.

## *Therapeutic Lens*

From a clinical perspective, *redemptive reframing* is very similar to what therapists call *cognitive restructuring* or *cognitive reframing*. Our brains create pathways around the stories we tell ourselves: "I failed," "I was rejected," or "Nothing good came from this." Those repeated thoughts shape how we feel in the present, even when the event is long over. When you begin to ask, "What did this teach me?" about the event or past pain instead of only "Why did this happen?" you are not denying the harm; you are interrupting an old way of thinking and building a new way of thinking. You are actually re-training the brain to become healthier. Over time, the brain learns to associate those memories with growth, wisdom, and boundaries rather than only shame and loss.

Spiritually, this is not simply positive thinking; it is partnering with Romans 8:28 and inviting God to reinterpret your story with you. In therapy, we might say, "Let's find a more truthful, balanced thought." In faith, we say, "Lord, show me where You were, and what You are forming in me through this."

Every stage of my healing—naming, wrestling, surrendering, releasing—had led to this one. The shift within me was both emotional and sacred. It was as if Heaven whispered, "Now you see." And when you see differently, you live differently.

## *Healing in Real Time*

One evening, after a particularly long hospital visit, I stopped by the chapel downstairs. The room was empty, lit only by the faint glow of a votive candle near the cross. I sat there, exhausted but aware of a sacred transformation happening within me.

For the first time, I didn't pray for God to fix anything. I simply said, "Thank You for trusting me with this part of the story."

Tears came, not from pain but from release. That prayer marked a pivot in my healing. Gratitude had replaced grief. Purpose had replaced pity. Compassion had replaced confusion. It was then that I truly understood that reframing is divine realignment. It means choosing to see through Heaven's lens, even when Earth's circumstances haven't fully changed.

## *Tools and Practices*

### Spiritual Tools

- Meditate on Romans 8:28. Ask: "Where might God be weaving good out of this specific wound?" Write in a journal one way your pain has already produced wisdom, empathy, or boundaries.
- Sit with Isaiah 61:3 and the promise of "beauty for ashes." Pray: "Lord, show me one 'ash' from my story and one small way You are turning it into testimony."
- Reflect on 2 Corinthians 12:9. Finish this sentence in prayer: "Lord, in this place of weakness, I see Your strength when…"

### Therapeutic Practices

- Draw two columns in a journal: "Old Story" and "New Story with God." For one painful memory, write the old narrative, then rewrite it through the lens of what it taught you.
- When you feel activated, ask: "What is this feeling trying to teach me about my needs, limits, or values?" Capture your answer in a sentence.
- Take a short walk or sit outdoors. As you notice the sky, trees, or sunset, quietly repeat: "Nothing is wasted. God, help

me see my life through Your lens." Let creation remind your nervous system that slow, steady change is holy too.

### *A Mutual Redemption*

When Red was discharged from the hospital, I helped coordinate his follow-up care. We sat together one last time before he returned home, the air filled with mutual respect and understanding. We talked not about what went wrong, but about what we had learned.

He said, "I never thought we would end up here—not like this. But I think this was God's way of humbling me. Of helping me see you again; not the way I wanted you to be, but the way you are."

That moment was unplanned grace. I didn't need an apology to validate my pain; his awareness was enough. Redemption doesn't always come wrapped in repentance. Sometimes, it comes clothed in recognition.

As I drove away, I realized something powerful: God had turned caregiving into closure, duty into destiny, and pain into perspective.

### *Framework Truth*

Redemptive reframing is the ability to hold your story in your hands and say, "This is what happened, but it is not who I am anymore." It's turning the ashes into an altar. Your scars don't disqualify you; they verify your survival. Your wounds don't weaken your witness; they deepen it. And your pain, when placed in God's hands, becomes a tool for transformation. That is the sacred shift; the moment healing becomes a part of your legacy.

### *The Forgiveness Framework™ – Integration of Identity*

Integration is forgiveness becoming part of the self rather than a moment of effort. It allows the past to exist without defining the present. In this stage, memory no longer triggers collapse, compassion no longer requires self-erasure, and boundaries no longer produce guilt.

Integration allows the heart to say, “This shaped me, but it does not define me.” Healing begins to weave itself into perception, leadership, relationships, and calling. Forgiveness becomes wisdom rather than weakness, a sense of strength expressed through peace. This integration reflects wholeness not because pain disappeared, but because it has been reframed, reconciled within the self, and entrusted to God’s purpose.

Framework 7

# Becoming the Leader You Needed

— ✦ —

***Healing is proven not by what you say, but by how you show up differently.***

During this stage, I stopped *doing* healing and started *being* healed. The striving gave way to stillness inside of me; the work became a way to heal, obey, and worship. The old reflexes that once braced me for disappointment began to quiet as my nervous system, my faith, and my soul learned a new rhythm: rest.

In the early phases of trying to forgive Red, every act of grace felt like labor. I journaled through tears, prayed through pain, and disciplined my mind to release past offenses when my heart still wanted justice. Yet, as this journey unfolded, forgiveness became less of an event and more of an atmosphere. The wounds that once governed my responses became reference points for wisdom rather than re-injury. I began to see that the point of healing was to integrate lessons learned into the narrative so that the narrative would be less painful and heavy to carry.

I no longer lived as the wounded one or the survivor. I lived as "the becoming one"—someone whose identity was being rebuilt on the other side of forgiveness.

## The Kiss That Healed Years of Hurt

I never imagined that a single kiss could compress a lifetime of pain, repentance, and redemption into one instant, but it did.

It began as an ordinary afternoon. Red had been cleared by the nurse for a short walk down the hospital corridor. The steady hum of monitors followed us as I wrapped my arm beneath his to steady his weakened frame. We moved slowly, step by step, through the sterile hallway.

Halfway down, he stopped beside a vending machine and leaned against the wall to catch his breath. I stood nearby, watchful, measuring the shallow pace of his breathing. Then he reached for my hand. My body instinctively stiffened. Old memories triggered the impulse to guard myself: *What does he want? What will this cost me?*

But his hand was gentle, his grasp unsteady; it was more searching than demanding. When our eyes met, something within me softened. There, in the hush between us, unspoken words swelled, filled with regret, apology, lingering affection, and maybe even mutual awe that after everything, grace had brought us back to this moment.

Slowly, he leaned forward and placed a kiss on my forehead. Not the controlling, performance-driven gestures of our past, but a trembling benediction, an offering of humility. The contact was light, but its message thundered through my spirit: *I'm sorry. I see you. I'm grateful.*

Tears poured down my cheeks instantly. The kiss didn't rewrite history, but it helped to reframe it. Years of personal anguish collapsed into a single exhale. That act became the physical manifestation of everything God had been teaching me: forgiveness is not amnesia; it's alchemy. It transforms pain into perspective and resentment into reverence for the healing process.

I wrapped my arms around him carefully, mindful of the IV line, and whispered a prayer of quiet gratitude. In that embrace, I came to a profound revelation: that sometimes healing doesn't roar; sometimes it sighs.

## Integration and the Rewired Brain

Daniel Siegel (2020) shared that a major hallmark of positive or efficient mental health is "integration," which is the synchronization of differentiated parts of one person into a functional whole. In trauma recovery, to oversimplify a little, this means that the amygdala (the part of the brain that processes emotions, including fear) quiets as the hippocampus (the part of the brain responsible for memory integration) and prefrontal cortex (the part of the brain that involves executive reasoning and impulse control) regain communication.

All this translated into the language of faith means that when going through the healing process, you're able to reintegrate all parts of yourself into a cohesive whole where, in part, your soul stops living in fight-or-flight and starts living in faith-and-flow.

Forgiveness is a neurological act as much as it is spiritual. When you choose empathy over anger, your brain releases oxytocin and serotonin, which can be considered to be biochemical affirmations of peace. Over time, this rewiring creates a baseline of calm where chaos once reigned.

Theologically, this is sanctification in the nervous system: holiness reaching all the synapses, which are firing properly.

## Leadership Application: Leading from Wholeness

The art of leadership can occur in marriages, board rooms, church congregations, and within so many other contexts. Being a leader is a role and not a job title. Leaders who operate from integration lead with integrity, which holds multiple meanings, one of them being "the state of being whole and undivided." A leader with integrity is not fractured by dual motives or masked by unresolved pain. They don't lead to prove; they lead to serve.

The hallmark of a servant leader is emotional intelligence. Psychologist Daniel Goleman's research for his 1995 book *Emotional Intelligence* identifies five core capacities of one who has developed competent emotional intelligence: self-awareness, self-regulation, motivation, empathy, and social skills. Forgiveness helps to cultivate each one.

- Self-awareness: You discern triggers without projecting them.
- Self-regulation: You respond thoughtfully rather than react on instinct.
- Motivation: Purpose, not ego, fuels your drive.
- Empathy: You perceive the person's needs beneath their poor behavior.
- Social skills: You build trust with others because, to them, your presence feels safe.

Healed leaders heal systems. Teams led by integrated leaders exhibit higher trust, lower turnover, and greater innovation because the team's perceived psychological safety flows from the leader's spiritual security.

Forgiveness, then, is not soft leadership; it is strategic leadership. It removes emotional reactivity and replaces it with responsiveness colored with critical thinking. You become a thermostat rather than a thermometer, setting the temperature of culture rather than mirroring it.

## Embodiment of Authenticity

Forgiveness turns you into a mirror that reflects grace in human form. You stop hiding your scars because they have become the credentials of your lived expertise. People don't follow perfection; they follow permission. Your transparency grants others the courage to heal. Being one's authentic self when following a leader who forgives no longer feels risky; it feels like the most responsible thing to do.

When you speak, your words hold weight because they are born of wholeness, not woundedness. You lead with a quiet authority that doesn't demand attention; it earns it.

As a leader who forgives, you are showing others hope and are living evidence that restoration is not simply a theory; it is actually possible.

## Red and the Redemptive Reframe

In clinical supervision within the world of therapeutic counseling, we often revisit pivotal encounters to examine transformation. That day in the corridor when Red kissed my forehead became a great case study in redemptive reframing. Through a trauma-informed lens, the kiss represented mutual acknowledgment of harm and the birth of secure closure. It allowed both parties to occupy the same emotional space without collapsing boundaries. Forgiveness was not dependency—it was differentiation with dignity.

Spiritually, it was a prophetic act. God allowed me to witness redemption embodied. It was a tangible metaphor for divine reconciliation. When I walked back to his room, my heart knew that is what integration looked like: remembering the past without resentment and loving without losing myself.

## Living as a Healed Leader

Integration doesn't end in introspection; it expresses itself through quality leadership. You begin to embody the capacity to translate personal healing into organizational and relational health. You lead meetings differently. You pause before reacting. You listen between the lines. You hold accountability and compassion in the same breath. You recognize that conflict is no longer a battlefield but a classroom. Your presence communicates stability to others. Your calm becomes contagious. When others encounter you, they sense something uncommon: an inner peace that's practiced and not performed for others.

## Identity Reconstruction: The New Narrative

Identity reconstruction means rewriting your internal script. The old narrative—"I am the one who was betrayed"—evolves into "I am the one who overcame." In narrative therapy, this is called re-authoring the story.

In kingdom language, this is your testimony. You begin to speak from the healed voice and not the hurt one. You own your story without letting it own you. You recognize that forgiveness didn't erase your identity but refined it.

Every role you hold in life, whether it's leader, parent, visionary, chaplain, or daughter of God, now operates from integration. There is no backstage self that you hide and no onstage persona that you perform. The same peace governs both. This is spiritual authenticity: when the person you are privately and the person you are publicly finally agree.

## Spiritual Reflection

### *Therapeutic Lens*

From a clinical perspective, what is happening in this stage of healing is *integration*. Parts of you that once felt split between two worlds, like the hurt child, hypervigilant protector, exhausted caregiver, or emerging wise adult, are beginning to work together instead of against each other. The nervous system shifts from constant threat-scanning into what therapists call a "window of tolerance," where you can feel big emotions without being swept away by them. You are no longer living only as the one who was wounded; you are living as the one who is being rebuilt.

Spiritually, this is what Scripture describes as renewal of the mind and sanctification of the heart. The Holy Spirit is not just comforting you; He is reorganizing your inner world around truth, safety, and grace. As integration grows, leadership flows more naturally from the wholeness that you are reclaiming. You don't have to perform or show everyone how strong you are; you *embody* it. Your healed nervous system becomes one more place where God's peace makes its home and shines so others can witness it.

## *Faith Declaration – Becoming Who God Designed You to Be*

In the Book of Genesis, God breathed into dust and called it "man." Every act of becoming is a replay of that divine inhalation, the Spirit of God animating a lifeless form. When forgiveness reconstructed your soul, God was breathing creation into your identity once more.

You are not just healed; you are re-created. You are not just restored; you are redefined. Using my experience as a metaphor in your own life, the kiss that once sealed sorrow has become the seal of transformation. You are the living proof that love resurrects what pain tried to bury.

## *Prayer of Integration*

"Father, Thank You for finishing what You started in me. Thank You that forgiveness didn't just free me; it formed me. Align my heart and mind so that my choices mirror Your wisdom. Let my leadership reflect healing and not hustle, as well as peace and not pressure. Teach me to move as one integrated being—whole, holy, and healed."

May my presence bring calm to myself and others, my words bring clarity, and my life bear fruit that leaves a lasting and positive legacy. Let every encounter with me be an encounter with grace. In Jesus' name, Amen.

## *Reflection and Action*

To maintain integration, therapists and spiritual directors often recommend engaging in grounding rituals that keep the body and soul in community and dialogue:

- Breathwork: be intentional about inhaling peace, then exhaling pressure.

- Somatic awareness: notice and try to pinpoint exactly where grace lives in your body.
- Reflective journaling: this is not to fix anything but to track and witness your growth.
- Forgiveness maintenance: engage in periodic check-ins with the heart—are there residues of bitterness hiding beneath new blessings?
- Community connection: surround yourself with people who mirror your healed identity and not your history.

These practices prevent relapse into reactive living. Integration, after all, is not a static state; it is a sustained synergy between faith, psychology, and embodiment.

### *Tools and Practices*

Spiritual Tools

- Read Romans 12:2 and ask: "Where am I still conforming to old survival roles, and how is God renewing my mind to lead from wholeness instead?"
- Read Colossians 3:15 and pray: "Lord, let Your peace be the umpire of my heart. Where is Your peace saying 'stay,' and where is it saying 'release'?"
- Read 2 Corinthians 12:9 and reflect: "How might God's strength show up in my softer, less-armored self today?"

Therapeutic Practices

- Gently scan your body from head to toe and name where you feel tension, softness, or calm. Thank God for each place that feels even slightly safe.
- Write a brief dialogue between "the old me" and "the becoming me," letting your healed voice reassure the part that still braces for harm.

- Choose one small action each day (a boundary, a rest, a kind word) that reflects the integrated leader you are becoming, and offer it to God as worship.

### *Forgiveness Decree – The Power of Becoming*

I decree that I am integrated—whole in spirit, soul, and body. Every fragmented memory aligns with divine harmony.

My past fuels wisdom and not warfare. My leadership flows from authenticity; my authority flows from alignment.

I am no longer reactive; I am responsive. I do not strive to become; I unfold what Heaven already declared.

I lead from peace, I live from purpose, and I love from overflow. Wholeness is my witness, and the legacy I leave behind is my language.

I legislate healing into every environment I enter. I am the embodiment of reconciliation—grace in motion. So let it be established on Earth as it is in Heaven.

### *The Becoming*

The kiss was the punctuation mark at the end of a long, painful sentence—and the capital letter of a brand-new paragraph. It symbolized the merging of pain meeting purpose, grief meeting grace, and shame meeting sacredness. That was my Becoming.

You, too, can have *your* Becoming. It is where your leadership, faith, and humanity intertwine. It is where healing stops being something you *have to* do and becomes something you *get* to do. It becomes habit. It is where forgiveness matures into wisdom, and wisdom becomes legacy.

In this place of Becoming and integration, you no longer live defined by what threatened to break you—you live defined by what built you after the hurt and pain. This is identity reconstruction. This is the wholeness you were always meant to embody. You have become the peace you once prayed for.

### *Framework Truth*

Becoming the leader you needed means living from integration. It is the courage to let God stitch together your story, your scars, and your strengths into one whole, undivided self. Your authority no longer comes from how loudly you perform but from how deeply you are aligned with God's will for your life. The same heart that once braced for impact now sets the temperature of every room you enter with safety, clarity, and grace. In God's hands, your healed identity becomes a covering for others, a living example that wholeness is possible and that leadership can flow from a soul at rest.

### *The Forgiveness Framework™ – Expanding Capacity for Wholeness*

In this stage, The Forgiveness Framework circles back to Capacity, but now in an expanded form. New capacity emerges as the heart learns healthier patterns of love, trust, discernment, and self-care. The nervous system no longer lives in constant vigilance; it begins to recognize safety. Emotional language grows stronger, allowing grief, anger, hope, and compassion to coexist without conflict. Capacity here is all about flourishing. It allows forgiveness to deepen without abandoning self-respect or relational clarity. As capacity widens, the soul becomes more anchored, more grounded, and more able to extend grace from a healed place. This is forgiveness that strengthens rather than drains.

Framework 8

# Leading From What You Survived

— ✦ —

***The healed version of you is the legacy the next generation is waiting for.***

This is the season of overflow, the rhythm of sustained healing. It is no longer a battle for you to become whole; it is a blessing to experience *becoming* whole. Peace is not a visitor in your life anymore; it lives inside you. It lingers in the spaces that once held tension. It hums quietly in the background of your daily life and is steady and grounding. What once triggered anxiety now invites reflection. What once reopened wounds now reminds you of how far grace has brought you.

Forgiveness is no longer an event or an effort. It is simply a part of your life. It moves through you like breath; you're able to inhale compassion and exhale release.

You no longer process offense the way you once did because your emotional architecture has changed. You have trained your spirit to return to equilibrium faster, to release without resentment, and to recover without the story of the wound becoming your identity.

This is what wholeness feels like when it matures. It's not perfection, but it will provide you with peace that positively impacts multiple parts of your life.

Song of Solomon 2:7 became a compass for me during my season of Becoming: "Do not awaken love until it so desires." Reconnecting with Red in the hospital was not about romance; it was about healing and finding the right rhythm between the two of us. It was about waiting for love of self, of God, and of another to awaken naturally and not prematurely forced by fear, loneliness, or nostalgia.

In earlier years, I mistook attention for affection and validation for value. But healed love moves differently than that. It doesn't chase; it chooses. It doesn't rush; it rests when it needs to.

## The Difference Between Desire and Need

There was a time I awakened love out of need to be seen, the need to belong, and the need to be chosen. Those "needs" led me to Red. At the time, I confused intensity for intimacy, charisma for character, and pursuit for partnership. My heart was tired, and tired hearts are easy prey for counterfeit love.

I once thought love was an exercise in endurance—holding on through dysfunction to prove my faithfulness to God and the covenant of marriage. But healed love knows that boundaries are sacred and not selfish, and that love should build up and not bruise.

Not long after my season of caring for Red, I met Adam. At this point, I had already made peace with solitude. I was not searching for completion through companionship; I was practicing contentment. My life was full already. I was spiritually alive, emotionally centered, and professionally purposeful. I had learned to enjoy the pace and flow of my own company.

So when Adam appeared, I didn't see him as a savior like I had with Red all those years ago; I saw him as an invitation to learn and grow. Yet, at first, I hesitated. My inner self couldn't help but wage a friendly battle between curiosity and caution. Part of me feared that opening my heart might dismantle the equilibrium I had fought so hard to protect. But another part, the healed part, told me that this would be different.

I remember one afternoon sitting on my porch, reading Song of Solomon again. My eyes lingered over the line: "Do not awaken love until it so desires." For the first time, I understood that passage as a covenant with peace. To not awaken love was to honor timing. It was to let God's alignment reveal what was real.

Because of that, I stopped trying to define the relationship. I held myself back from rushing toward outcomes. Adam and I let things unfold in divine order: slowly, prayerfully, and intentionally.

This was not love born out of scarcity; it was love born of a surplus from a healed heart that no longer needed rescue.

## Learning to Love from Wholeness

There is a difference between falling in love and standing in love. Falling implies loss of balance; standing implies stability. With Adam, I learned to stand.

We spent months simply talking, listening, and praying. There was laughter, but also silence, which wasn't awkward at all but peaceful. Neither of us pretended to anything but ourselves. We showed up, raw and honest, without any metaphorical makeup on our souls. In earlier seasons of life, I might have rushed ahead, scripting the future before the foundation was tested. With Adam, I trusted the process more than the projection.

Healing had rewired my relational reflexes. I no longer needed constant affirmation to feel secure. My identity wasn't anchored in someone's affection; it was rooted in God's approval. One evening, Adam said something that sealed this truth: "You carry peace like it's furniture; you walk into a room, and it rearranges the atmosphere."

I smiled because I knew what it cost me to attain that level of inner peace. It came from nights of wrestling, years of forgiving, and the courage to walk away from codependency disguised as a Godly covenant.

Forgiveness had not just healed my past; it had expanded my capacity to love purely, freely, and wisely. I learned that when love awakens in alignment with God's timing, it doesn't trigger anxiety; it produces assurance. It doesn't require you to shrink; it invites you to shine.

## Spiritual Reflection

Healing isn't maintained by miracles but by steady habits. This stage of healing brought abundance in my life, which taught me that peace must be practiced, not just proclaimed. Wholeness is sustained through daily disciplines that keep the heart uncluttered and the mind renewed. Here are five that I recommend:

1. The Habit of Stillness – I learned to start my mornings in quiet reflection before checking messages or managing schedules. Stillness became a daily sanctuary where God recalibrated my perspective before the world could demand my energy.
2. The Habit of Gratitude – Gratitude became my language of abundance. Each night, I named three things I was thankful for. This habit trained my eyes to notice grace in the ordinary, like the way sunlight hit my journal, the scent of coffee, or an unexpected text from a friend.
3. The Habit of Boundaries – Boundaries didn't disappear with healing; they matured. Now they served not to keep people out, but to keep peace in. I guarded my time, my energy, and my emotional bandwidth with great diligence.
4. The Habit of Reflection – Healing deepens through reflection. Every month, I ask myself: *Where am I thriving? Where am I avoiding? What is God trying to teach me now?* This self-inquiry kept me accountable to growth rather than allowing complacency to take over.
5. The Habit of Service – True wholeness overflows into service. I found renewed joy in mentoring women, leading workshops, and writing books that turned my private healing into public hope.

Each time I poured out, I noticed that peace multiplied and never depleted.

These habits became my spiritual architecture, keeping my inner home uncluttered and my soul rooted in truth.

### *Therapeutic Lens*

In trauma recovery, clinicians often describe healing as a shift from *survival responses* to *regulation responses*. Prior to awareness due to recovery, the nervous system reacts quickly to perceived threats, especially relational ones, because past wounds trained the body to brace for painful conflict. But in your current season of healing and overflow, your system has learned a new rhythm because it has become aware when the nervous system is on high alert. What once activated hypervigilance now activates reflection. This is a sign of emotional integration or wholeness: your brain is no longer scanning for danger, but for context and meaning around what's currently happening.

From a therapeutic standpoint, healthy love becomes possible only when internal safety has been restored. You are no longer seeking connection from a place of fear or deficit; you are relating from a place of mental and emotional stability. Spiritually, this mirrors Song of Solomon 2:7, waiting for love to awaken naturally rather than from panic, loneliness, or longing. Wholeness means your body and spirit have learned to trust that the peace you're feeling is actually safe. And from that place, discernment becomes clearer, timing becomes gentler, and love becomes sustainable.

### *Tools and Practices*

#### Spiritual Tools

- Reflect on Song of Solomon 2:7. Ask: "Lord, where are You inviting me to wait for love, timing, or direction instead of awakening something prematurely?" Write in your journal one place in your life where patience protects your peace.

- Meditate on Isaiah 26:3: "You will keep in perfect peace those whose minds are stayed on You." Journal what currently anchors your peace and what distracts you from it.
- Sit with Philippians 1:6. Pray: "God, show me the ways You are completing the healing work in me." Note in your journal one area where spiritual growth has softened an old reflex.

Therapeutic Practices

- Write down three internal signals that show you are operating from wholeness (e.g., calm decision-making, stable boundaries, reduced fear of loss). Use this before entering new relational spaces.
- Identify one personal value, like peace, honesty, or rest, and ask: "Did my choices today honor this value?" This supports alignment rather than emotional reactivity.
- When relational anxiety shows up, note the trigger, the old wound it reflects, and the new truth you're living from. This reinforces nervous-system regulation and spiritual alignment.

### *Case Study: Helping Others Heal from Need-Based Love*

One of my coaching clients, Tanya, mirrored much of my former self. She had spent years chasing love that hurt her. Her pattern was predictable: attract emotionally unavailable partners, confuse pursuit with passion, and abandon her boundaries in the name of faith.

When she entered my program, she poured her heart out and exclaimed through tears, "Dr. Burke, I just don't understand why God keeps letting me love people who break me."

I smiled gently and replied, "Sometimes it's not that God is sending the wrong people; it's that we are awakening love before it's ready. Healing has its own clock."

Together, we unpacked the difference between attachment and alignment. She learned to identify her triggers, to sit with discomfort instead of rushing into distraction. Gradually, she began cultivating the same peace I had fought for, one decision at a time.

Months later, she sent me a message that made me choke up a little: "For the first time, I'm not lonely. I'm alone, but I'm not empty. I think I finally get what you mean by living in overflow."

That message confirmed that when you live healed, your wholeness becomes contagious. You become evidence that peace is possible.

## *Legacy and Sustained Peace*

Overflow is not excess; it is evidence that you have been faithful to your healing, that forgiveness works, and that God restores what trauma tried to steal from you.

In this stage, your healing ceases to be about survival and becomes about stewardship. You begin to hold onto peace in spaces still battling storms. You no longer need to prove transformation because you embody it.

You have become the healed leader, the living testimony that emotional intelligence, spiritual depth, and forgiveness are not competing forces but collaborative ones. You are leading, loving, and living from the center and not the edge.

Even your presence preaches now. You don't have to speak to shift the atmosphere of rooms you enter; your energy does it for you. Your peace has a gravity to it. Your forgiveness has a sweet and inviting fragrance. Your joy has the air of empathetic authority.

You understand that legacy is not what you leave behind; it is what flows through you daily. It's the compassion you extend, the wisdom you impart, the boundaries you model, and the love you give without losing yourself.

The story with Adam, whether it continued or simply served its divine purpose, became a reflection of the truth that you can love again, not because you forgot what broke you, but because you remember Who healed you.

### *The Rhythm of Wholeness*

This stage is not about perfection but cultivating a sense of peace practiced in real time. Forgiveness becomes your default language. Grace becomes your instinct. You no longer live from reaction; you live from revelation. This is legacy living in the moment. This is sustained wholeness.

You are no longer the woman searching for closure; you are the woman creating it. You are no longer the one begging for peace; you are the one breathing it into rooms. Your forgiveness journey has matured into overflow and abundance.

And your story, a legacy of forgiveness, has become an open invitation for others to begin their own path toward forgiveness and healing. Because in the end, wholeness was never just about you. It was also about the countless hearts your healing would awaken.

### *Reflection and Action*

- What does "overflow" look like in your current season?
- Where do you feel peace multiplying rather than being depleted?
- How can your healed presence create safety and transformation for others?

### *Framework Truth*

Forgiveness, when sustained, becomes legacy. Wholeness, when practiced, becomes peace that multiplies. And love, when awakened in God's timing, becomes rooted in self-knowledge and inner peace.

### *The Forgiveness Framework™ – Integration as Influence*

Here, Integration is now expressed in community, leadership, and generational impact. Forgiveness becomes visible not only in private healing but in how one leads, responds, nurtures, and builds relationships. Integrated forgiveness models boundaries without bitterness, compassion without codependency, and strength without hardness. It reshapes relational culture by replacing reaction with grounding, rigidity with grace, and endurance-at-all-costs with wisdom. Integration here becomes legacy-forming; it shifts dynamics that once repeated pain and replaces them with healthier patterns of connection and stability. This level of forgiveness allows healing within one's life to begin to ripple outward.

Framework 9

# Legacy that Outlives the Wound

—✦—

***Forgiveness is not about rewriting the past; it is about reclaiming your future.***

Not too long ago, I remember sitting in my therapist's office on that familiar beige couch. My notebook was open, but my pen wasn't moving. I felt stuck, like my thoughts were trapped in a loop, circling the same old stories I had told a hundred times before.

My therapist leaned forward and looked at me with the kind of gaze that made me feel both exposed and safe. "Ansonya," she said, choosing her words carefully, "you wear grittiness and loyalty like a jacket."

I frowned. "What do you mean?" I asked.

She tilted her head slightly. "You wear these things like a badge. You think staying in challenging places and relationships longer than you should makes you faithful. You believe pushing through suffering proves how strong you are. But sometimes armor can become your prison."

Her words pierced through my practiced composure. Suddenly, memories of my past came rushing in; there were relationships I stayed in even when they drained me, ministry roles I clung to long after God had released me from them, and situations where I mistook endurance for obedience to Scripture.

I sat there stunned, with tears welling up. For years, I had praised myself for what I thought was resilience—the ability to bounce back from challenging situations. It's a kind of toughness. Others praised me for this "toughness" too. I had learned to survive storms, to keep standing no matter how fierce the winds blew. But what I thought was strength had become a disguise for bondage.

In that moment, I realized that toughness and grit, when untethered from discernment, can become self-sabotage. That session stripped me bare. I began to see the layers beneath my "strong woman" identity. Being resilient or tough had become my identity; it was a label I wore with pride, even when it was destroying me. I realized now that survival had replaced actual healing; I was functioning and not flourishing. I learned how the idea of loyalty had kept me trapped in cycles God never intended for me to endure.

I wrestled with the shame of realizing I had confused bondage for bravery. But I also felt the first stirrings of freedom from the "resilient" or "tough" label I thought I had to embody. Naming it gave me power to change.

Forgiveness, I realized, would require me to peel off that jacket—piece by piece—until I could feel again. It wasn't that being tough or gritty was bad; it was that I had used it as armor to avoid vulnerability.

Armor serves a purpose in battle, but when the war is over, and you're still wearing it, it becomes too heavy, making it difficult for you to function properly. And if you wear the armor too long, you forget what softness feels like.

## The Nature of Resistance

Nobody tells you that forgiveness fights back. People love the "just forgive and move on" cliché, but forgiveness doesn't unfold that easily. Resistance to forgiveness isn't failure either; it's part of the process.

Therapists call this ambivalence, or the clash between wanting freedom and fearing it. Spiritually, it mirrors Jesus in Gethsemane, uttering,

"Not my will, but Yours be done" (Luke 22:42). That's what forgiveness feels like: a spiritual wrestling match between flesh and spirit.

Resistance can show up in sneaky ways, like in the tightness in your chest when the perpetrator's name comes up, anger at the thought of letting them "off the hook," fear that forgiving means letting them back in, or a deep sense of injustice that says, "If I forgive, who will pay for what they did?"

Naming resistance is not weakness; it's honesty. And honesty is the soil of healing. When I began admitting to God that I didn't want to forgive, that I didn't feel safe, and that I was tired of being the "bigger person," my perspective on it all shifted. The honesty itself became a doorway. Forgiveness didn't start with a feeling; it started with a choice to surrender the right to revenge and trust God with the results.

## Research Insights

Forgiveness research confirms what both Scripture and experience reveal: resistance is normal and expected. Ambivalence is common. Studies show people often hold both desires to forgive and to hold on simultaneously. Normalizing this paradox reduces shame.

False resilience backfires. Research finds that rigid endurance (like me for so many years, staying rooted in relationships that did not serve me) increases burnout and decreases well-being, while adaptive resilience—resilience with flexibility and boundaries—improves emotional health and leadership capacity.

Forgiveness heals. A 2022 meta-analysis found forgiveness interventions significantly reduced depression, anxiety, and hostility, while increasing hope and life satisfaction.

Forgiveness work, then, is not linear. It's iterative: two steps forward and one step back. It's spiritual rehab. And that's why God's grace is essential; because you can't muscle your way through forgiveness; you have to heal your way through it.

## Leadership Lens

Leaders fall into the trap of false resilience all the time. We stay in toxic environments because endurance has been mislabeled as loyalty. We preach perseverance while privately bleeding. We keep dysfunctional systems alive because we confuse silence with strength.

But unhealed leaders replicate their pain. Teams mirror what they see modeled. If we mistake bondage for bravery, we will reproduce exhaustion instead of freedom. Resilient leadership isn't about how much you can take; it's about how well you can adapt.

True resilience says, "I can't control what happened, but I can control how I respond and what I bring into the future." Leaders who learn this difference embody grace and not grit. They create cultures where vulnerability isn't punished, where rest isn't weakness, and where forgiveness becomes part of organizational DNA.

When I began leading from a healed place instead of a hurt place, I noticed a change in my perspective and in the energy I brought into every room. Meetings felt lighter. Collaboration replaced competition. Compassion became policy. I began to realize that when a healed leader walks in, the entire atmosphere changes.

## Legacy Lens

Sitting on that couch in my therapist's office that day, I had a sobering realization: if I didn't take this armor off, I would hand it to the next generation. My children, my mentees, and my spiritual daughters would learn that loyalty means never leaving, even when it costs you your peace. That suffering silently is proof of love. That boundaries are something others can violate time and time again. That is not the legacy I want to leave behind.

Legacy, I've learned, isn't what you build—it's what you model. The next generation learns not from what you preach but from what you practice.

And so, I made a decision that I would redefine resilience for them. I would show them that faithfulness doesn't mean self-abandonment, that strength includes softness, and that saying "no" can be as holy as saying "yes."

## Spiritual Reflection

### *Aha Nuggets*

- Resilience without healing is armor. Resilience with healing is wisdom.
- If resilience keeps you chained, it isn't strength; it's survival masquerading as faithfulness.

### *When Shadows Arise*

As freeing as this revelation was for me, it didn't erase my past. Healing has a way of exposing new layers just when you think you've "arrived."

Even as I began walking in greater peace, shadows from my past occasionally reappeared. A raised voice from Adam, even if it was just enthusiasm about a game on TV, could make my pulse race. A canceled plan could trigger an old sense of abandonment.

Sometimes, I snapped at him for small things, bracing for conflict that never came. But the difference this time was my awareness. I recognized these reactions as echoes of past trauma and not reflections of present reality.

Instead of hiding from them, I named them. "I'm sorry I overreacted," I told him once, "this kind of situation brings up memories from my past."

Each time, Adam responded with empathy instead of defensiveness, reinforcing what I was learning: real love creates a safe space for vulnerability.

I also brought these moments to therapy. I wanted to make sure I didn't let old wounds sabotage new possibilities. The work was humbling, but it taught me something crucial: I wasn't looking for a perfect man; I was cultivating a healthy dynamic with myself and my potential partner. I was building a strong foundation.

### *Prepared for Real Love*

Through this unfolding process, God began to prepare my heart for a different kind of love, one anchored in peace and not adrenaline. For years, I had mistaken chaos for passion. The rollercoaster made me feel alive, but it was really anxiety masquerading as romance. Healing recalibrated my definition of love.

This new season felt slower and steadier. It was love that celebrated mutual flourishing. I understood now that even if Adam wasn't "the one," this relationship was healthy practice; a proving ground for wholeness.

And if he was part of God's plan, I was learning how to walk wisely toward it. When we finally had an open conversation about our future, he said, "I care deeply for you. I respect your pace. I want to explore what God is doing between us—without any pressure."

With Adam, I felt safe enough to share my non-negotiables, such as my daughter's well-being, my peace, and fulfilling my purpose. He listened with sincerity, nodding thoughtfully. "I want the same kind of stable, God-centered love," he said.

That exchange marked a milestone. For the first time in years, I felt aligned emotionally, spiritually, and relationally. The old me would have been swept up in fantasy. The healed me was grounded in discernment. Whether Adam became my life partner or simply a chapter in my story, I had learned the greater lesson that healing prepares you to love from a place of wholeness and not a wounded place.

### *The Resilient Heart*

Resilience used to mean pushing through, no matter what. Now it means standing firm without hardening. It means acknowledging that triggers may still come, but they don't own me anymore. It means that fear might creep up on me, but faith speaks louder. It means remembering that healing doesn't erase scars, but it does mean it redeems them.

Every time I choose honesty over pretending, boundaries over people-pleasing, or rest over relentless striving, I reclaim another piece of my peace.

This is the kind of resilience that leads to a lasting legacy; the kind that protects peace instead of performance and that honors self-worth instead of self-sacrifice.

I now embody resilience differently. Not as armor, but as adornment. Not as something to hide behind, but as evidence of grace. And in this, I finally understood that resilience is not about surviving everything; it is about knowing when you no longer have to.

## *Therapeutic Lens*

From a clinical perspective, what happened in that therapist's office is known as *identity deconstruction,* which is the moment a person realizes that a once-protective coping strategy has become a barrier to present-day healing. Many trauma survivors adopt "grit," overfunctioning, or hyper-loyalty like a protective coating, because these behaviors once helped them survive unpredictable environments. But when the nervous system stays in chronic resilience mode, it cannot access vulnerability, connection, or rest. Therapy teaches that recognizing this ambivalence, wanting freedom yet fearing what it requires, is progress. Insight breaks the illusion that enduring trauma equals emotional safety.

Spiritually, this reflects God's invitation in Ezekiel 36:26: "I will remove your heart of stone and give you a heart of flesh." Healing softens what trauma hardened. As you release false resilience and embrace honest vulnerability, your body learns safety, your spirit learns surrender, and your legacy shifts from surviving pain to transforming it into something meaningful.

## *Tools and Practices*

### Spiritual Tools

- Reflect on Ezekiel 36:26: Pray, "Lord, show me one place where my heart has become stone from survival." Write down what compassion, boundaries, or rest might look like in that area.
- Read Luke 22:42 and reflect on Jesus in Gethsemane. Ask, "Where am I wrestling between what I want and what healing requires?" Journal the tension honestly without judgment.
- Go to Psalm 139:23-24: Invite God to reveal hidden patterns. "Search me… and show me the ways I still wear armor You are asking me to lay down." Note any emotions or memories that surface.

Therapeutic Practices

- Write in your journal three "protective behaviors" you use (overfunctioning, staying loyal too long, minimizing hurt). Next to each, write what that behavior once protected and what it now costs you.
- In your journal, draw two circles labeled "What wants to heal" and "What is afraid to heal." List thoughts or fears in each. This normalizes resistance and builds self-awareness.
- Identify one small behavior you want the next generation to learn from you, such as setting a boundary or using your voice. Practice it once this week as an intentional act of healing-in-motion.

## *Framework Truth*

Crafting a personal legacy that outlives past wounds means choosing to let God write the last line of your story and not the person who hurt you. Resilience without healing hands your armor to the next generation; resilience with healing provides them with tools to develop wisdom, boundaries, and peace for themselves. In this place of healing, you no longer have to prove how much you can endure; you get to model what it looks like to be whole. When you lay down false toughness and forgive from a healed heart, you do more than survive your story; you change the story your children and spiritual sons and daughters will tell many years from now.

### *The Forgiveness Framework™ – Legacy of Release and Integration*

In this stage, Forgiveness matures into a way of being, rooted in discernment, compassion, and truth. Release removes the authority of old wounds, while integration ensures that resilience is expressed as wisdom rather than armor. This is forgiveness that transforms survival into inheritance, shaping how we love, lead, parent, and walk with God. It does not hand future generations the burden of unresolved pain; it hands them language, boundaries, tenderness, and peace. Here, forgiveness does not erase history but redeems its influence. The story no longer ends at the wound; it continues through the healing God cultivated within.

Final Thoughts

# From Armor to Anointing

—✦—

***You are not responsible for rewriting the past, but you are entrusted with shaping what comes next.***

That beige couch moment in therapy became a defining line between who I was and who I was becoming. In taking off the armor, I found a softness that I needed to learn to be vulnerable enough to let new and healthy love into my life. A love that trusts God more than control and that allows joy to coexist with memory and peace to coexist with past pain.

Every restored and redeemed leader, woman, and story begins at the point when they learn to forgive from a healed place, taking off the armor that no longer protects but imprisons. They own what once hurt them, walking in empowerment, using the past to help others heal in the present. They stop proving that they're strong and start living like they're free. That freedom, that inner peace, is something available to everyone—even you.

If you have made it this far into this book, I want you to pause for a moment and honor that. Exploring these pages is not passive work. You have allowed yourself to look within yourself at places that once felt unsafe, unanswered, or unresolved. That alone is an act of courage. You may not feel "finished," but healing does not require a finish line to be real. Sometimes the bravest thing you can say is, "I am still becoming."

There will be days when forgiveness feels strong in you, and others when old memories try to reclaim ground. Do not interpret that as failure. Healing is never a straight line. The fact that you returned here again and again means something in you is choosing peace over bitterness, truth over denial, and freedom over familiar pain.

Now comes the challenge. Do not keep this work private. Legacy is never built in isolation. What you practice in private will show up in public, in your relationships, in your leadership, and in your children's nervous systems. Forgiveness that stays hidden will heal you, but forgiveness that is integrated will heal generations. Choose one place in your life where you will live differently because of what you have learned here. One conversation. One boundary. One prayer spoken with honesty instead of performance.

You are not responsible for rewriting the past, but you are entrusted with shaping what comes next. The wound may have been your beginning, but it does not have to be your conclusion. Let forgiveness become your inheritance and your offering. Your legacy is already in motion.

With blessings,

Ansonya

Afterword

# Jamal Vallair

A Unresolved disappointment, betrayal, and breached trust—internal strain that has been managed but never addressed—eventually show up in decision-making, boundaries, culture, and performance.

Forgiveness is rarely named as the issue, yet it often sits at the center of the breakdown.

What Dr. Ansonya Burke offers in this work is something few leaders are actually equipped to do well: approaching forgiveness with both emotional intelligence and structural integrity. Not as spiritual bypassing. Not as emotional obligation. But as a disciplined, trauma-informed process that restores internal clarity and leadership capacity.

I know Dr. Burke as a leader who does not speak in theory. When she made the decision to return and care for her former husband after years of betrayal and separation, it was not naïveté—it was obedience informed by therapy, discernment, and boundary clarity. That lived courage gives this book its weight.

This work matters now because many leaders are functional but fragmented. They've learned how to perform through depletion and normalize inner tension as the price of responsibility. Dr. Burke gives language to what leaders feel but rarely articulate: unresolved inner conflict quietly erodes trust, clouds judgment, and compromises sustainability

The Forgiveness Framework is not a motivational concept. It is a nine-step, research-backed process that moves leaders from personal healing to organizational impact to legacy. Dr. Burke connects what most treat as separate: internal wholeness and external influence. This book addresses not only how to heal, but how to lead from that healing in ways that shape culture, strengthen trust, and establish what you leave behind.

This is not a book designed to convince you that forgiveness matters. It assumes you already know that. Instead, it offers a responsible framework—one that respects pace, capacity, and discernment.

If you've done the work externally but still feel unresolved internal load, this book is an invitation—not to revisit pain, but to remove what no longer has the right to drive your leadership.

– Jamal Vallair

Neuroscience Performance & Leadership Coach | United States Navy, 20 Years Retired

www.ingramcontent.com/pod-product-compliance
Lightning Source LLC
LaVergne TN
LVHW010935110826
845149LV00013B/2612
* 9 7 9 8 9 9 5 3 5 0 8 9 7 *